ANGELA HARTNETT

A TASTE OF HOME

ANGELA HARTNETT

A TASTE OF HOME

200 QUICK AND EASY RECIPES

EBURY
PRESS

10 9 8 7 6 5 4 3 2 1

Published in 2011 by Ebury Press, an imprint of Ebury Publishing

Ebury Publishing is a division of the Random House Group

The Random House Group Limited Reg. No. 954009

Addresses for companies within the Random House Group can be found
at www.randomhouse.co.uk

A CIP catalogue record for this book is available from the British Library

The Random House Group Limited makes every effort to ensure that
the papers used in our books are made from trees that have been legally
sourced from well-managed and credibly certified forests. Our paper
procurement policy can be found on www.randomhouse.co.uk/environment

Designed and typeset by Smith & Gilmour, London
Printed and bound in China by C&C Offset Printing Co., Ltd

ISBN 978-0-09-193339-5

CONTENTS

INTRODUCTION

For me, home cooking is more about sharing good meals with friends than showing off cheffy skills. If you're having people over for a meal you want to spend time with them, not chained to the kitchen, so you need recipes that are easy and enjoyable to cook. Cooking should be fun, not stressful, so don't get too anxious about it all. Mistakes happen to the best of us – me included – and as my mum says, you can always go and get a curry if you overcook the meat and burn the apple tart!

The recipes in this book are for the kind of food I like to eat at home – simple, tasty and not too complicated to make at the end of a working day. These are dishes I enjoy cooking for friends and include some of my favourite foods – Macaroni cheese, Steak salad, Figs with vanilla ice cream and Chicken noodle soup.

You won't need to spend precious time hunting down exotic ingredients. Nearly everything is readily available at supermarkets and farmers' markets. There are recipes you can make from leftovers, too, and many are very easily adapted to suit the contents of your larder. Of course my inherited love of Italian food is evident so there has to be a chapter on pasta and risotto. No cookbook is complete without these in my opinion! But I've included some slightly different variations that you may not have come across before, such as Spaghetti with mussels and Chestnut and truffle risotto.

I'm lucky in having friends who are great cooks and I've begged and borrowed recipes I've enjoyed at their houses. There's my neighbour's Beef with butternut squash and my friend Liz's fantastic Banana bread to name just a couple of these fantastic dishes. I've included quite a few cakes, too, as home baking is always hugely popular – there's nothing like a home-made cake. When my mum hears about some great chef she often remarks: 'All very well, but can he bake a cake?'

So I hope you enjoy these recipes and have fun trying something different. And feel free to adapt and change to suit your taste – that's always when the best dishes happen.

NOTES

All olive oil is extra virgin

All butter is unsalted unless specified otherwise

All eggs are large, organic and free-range unless specified otherwise

Herbs should be fresh if possible, unless dried herbs are specified

All fresh herbs, fruit and vegetables should be washed before use

All milk is full-fat unless specified otherwise

All onions, shallots and garlic should be peeled unless specified otherwise

All lemons should be unwaxed

I like to use Maldon sea salt but occasionally a recipe may refer to rock salt

SNACKS

DEEP-FRIED SQUID

This is a quick, easy snack and perfect party food.

200g cornflour
100g rice flour
40g garlic powder
good pinch of salt
pinch of cayenne pepper
pinch of Szechuan pepper
300g baby squid, cleaned
    and cut into rings
vegetable or sunflower oil,
    for deep-frying
squeeze of fresh lemon juice

SERVES 4

MIX THE CORNFLOUR with the rest of the dry ingredients in a large bowl.

TOSS THE SQUID in the flour mixture until evenly coated, shaking off any excess.

HEAT THE OIL to 180°C in a deep-fat fryer or heavy-based pan and fry the baby squid for 2–3 minutes, until golden brown. Drain well on kitchen paper and serve immediately with a squeeze of fresh lemon juice.

MARINATED SEA BREAM

An economical alternative to sea bass, bream is a versatile fish
and can be served as carpaccio, pan-fried or oven-baked.

4 sea bream fillets,
   skinned and pin-boned
3 blood oranges
3 tbsp olive oil
soy sauce (optional)
4 breakfast radishes, sliced
½ bunch watercress, leaves
   picked from the stems
small bunch of coriander,
   leaves picked from
   the stems
1 tsp sesame seeds
salt and freshly ground
   black pepper

SERVES 4

SLICE THE SEA BREAM at an angle into thick slices. Peel 2 of
the blood oranges and divide them into segments. Cut the third
orange in half and squeeze out the juice.

MIX 2 TABLESPOONS of blood orange juice with the olive oil
to make a vinaigrette and add a dash of soy sauce if desired.

PUT A LITTLE OF THE BLOOD ORANGE MIXTURE on a plate, add
the bream and season. Then pour on the rest of the juice mixture
and leave the fish for 3–4 minutes.

GARNISH with the orange segments, radish slices, watercress,
coriander and sesame seeds, then serve immediately.

CLAMS WITH CHORIZO AND ROCKET

These sensational Spanish flavours transport you
straight to the bars of Barcelona.

2 tbsp olive oil
500g clams, washed
splash of white wine
1 garlic clove, sliced
1 thyme sprig
2 baby shallots,
    sliced into rings
100g chorizo
1 bag of rocket leaves
1 tbsp chopped flatleaf
    parsley
salt and freshly ground
    black pepper

SERVES 4

HEAT A HEAVY-BASED PAN over a medium heat and add the
olive oil. Throw in the clams with the white wine, garlic, thyme
and shallots. Put a lid on the pan and steam until the clams
are cooked – about 5 minutes.

STRAIN everything into a big bowl, discarding any clams that don't
open. Keep the cooking juices and serve them with the salad.

SLICE THE CHORIZO and fry in a little olive oil for 1 minute, then
add to the clams. Finish with the rocket and parsley and season to
taste. Good served with some toasted sourdough bread.

CRAB FRITTERS

These are a delicious starter and a perfect way of using British crab.

1 egg
50g self-raising flour
vegetable oil, for deep-frying
½ tsp finely chopped
   red chilli
1 spring onion, chopped
200g white crabmeat
1 tbsp chopped fresh
   coriander
1 lime, cut into wedges,
   for serving
salt and freshly ground
   black pepper

SERVES 2-4

BEAT THE EGG AND FLOUR together to make a batter. Heat a little of the vegetable oil in a frying pan and fry the chilli and spring onion until softened. Tip them into a bowl and leave to cool.

ADD THE CRABMEAT to the cooled chilli and spring onion, season and add the coriander. Stir in the egg and flour, then if the mixture seems a little dry, add a tablespoon of water to bind everything together.

SHAPE THE MIXTURE into fritters each about the size of a golf ball. Heat the oil in a large pan or deep-fat fryer to 180°C. Fry the fritters in batches until golden and drain on kitchen paper.

SERVE THE FRITTERS with lime wedges or some yoghurt mixed with a little chopped dill.

SARDINES ON TOAST

1 tsp capers
1 red onion, finely chopped
2 tomatoes, chopped
1 tsp chopped basil
1 tsp chopped flatleaf
    parsley
grated zest of 1 lemon
1 tbsp olive oil
8 sardines, filleted and
    pin-boned
4 slices of sourdough bread,
    toasted
squeeze of fresh lemon juice
salt and freshly ground
    black pepper

SERVES 4

MIX THE CAPERS with the chopped onion, tomatoes, herbs and lemon zest to make a marinade. Season to taste and set aside.

HEAT THE OLIVE OIL in a pan and fry the sardines for 2 minutes. Alternatively, put them on a grill pan, season with a little oil and salt and cook them under the grill.

SPREAD SOME OF THE CAPER MIXTURE over the slices of toasted sourdough. Add the sardines, then cover with the rest of the caper mixture. Serve immediately with a squeeze of lemon.

FRIED DUCK EGGS
ON TOAST

100g mixed wild
    mushrooms
knob of butter
handful of wild garlic,
    chopped
2 duck eggs
2 pieces of focaccia
salt and freshly ground
    black pepper

SERVES 2

WIPE THE MUSHROOMS or wash them gently if very dirty, then trim and slice them.

MELT HALF THE BUTTER in a pan and sauté the mushrooms until tender but not soggy. Add the wild garlic, cook for 30 seconds, then switch off the heat and leave the mushrooms and garlic in the pan while you cook the eggs.

HEAT THE REST OF THE BUTTER in a non-stick frying pan and fry the duck eggs for 3–4 minutes, or until cooked to your liking.

GRILL THE FOCACCIA on one side. Pile some mushrooms and garlic onto the toasted side of the focaccia and top with the eggs. Season the eggs and serve.

SALMON TARTARE

Make sure you use the freshest salmon for this dish and
serve it nicely chilled (see picture opposite).

300g fresh salmon fillet,
skinned and pin-boned
juice and grated zest of
1 lime
1 tsp chives
1 tsp chervil
4 tsp crème fraîche
crispbread or toasted rye
bread, for serving
salt and freshly ground
black pepper

SERVES 3–4

FINELY CHOP THE SALMON FLESH. Gently mix the salmon, lime
juice and zest, herbs and crème fraîche in a bowl and season to
taste. Add more lime or pepper as desired.

CHILL SLIGHTLY and serve with crispbread or toasted rye bread.

BEEF TARTARE

Make this as mild or spicy as you like by adding more or less of the
seasoning. You can add a dash of ketchup, too, for a sweet spicy taste.

500g beef fillet, diced
1 shallot, finely diced
1 tbsp Worcestershire sauce
3–4 shakes of Tabasco sauce
1 tsp grated horseradish
1 tbsp olive oil
grilled sourdough bread,
for serving
salt and freshly ground
black pepper

SERVES 4–6

PUT THE BEEF in a bowl with the shallot and add Worcestershire
sauce and Tabasco to taste. Finish with the grated horseradish,
olive oil and seasoning.

SERVE with grilled sourdough.

CHICKEN AND WATERCRESS SANDWICH

This is a great way to use up leftover roast chicken. Spice up the mayo with a touch of chilli powder if you like.

roast chicken
garlic mayonnaise
squeeze of fresh lemon juice
2 slices of sourdough bread
½ ripe avocado, sliced
chopped tarragon or
    watercress
salt and freshly ground
    black pepper

SERVES 1

SHRED THE CHICKEN INTO LARGE CHUNKS and mix with a touch of garlic mayonnaise and a squeeze of lemon.

TOAST THE SOURDOUGH. Spread the chicken mixture onto one piece of toast and add some slices of avocado and a sprinkling of tarragon or watercress. Season and top with the other piece of sourdough.

PORK SANDWICHES

For a slightly different version, use softer bread and heat the pork through in the oven. Add the mayo and soy sauce to the hot sandwich.

2–3 tbsp mayonnaise
1 tbsp soy sauce
juice of 1 lime
1 tbsp picked coriander
    leaves
1 French stick
200g roast pork, sliced
salt and freshly ground
    black pepper

SERVES 3-4

MIX THE MAYONNAISE with the soy sauce, lime juice and coriander leaves. Split the French stick in half lengthways and spread the mayonnaise mixture over the cut surface of both halves of the bread.

ADD THE SLICES OF ROAST PORK to one half, season, then top with the other piece of bread. Slice into about 4 pieces and serve.

BEEF ON GRILLED SOURDOUGH

There are plenty of great bakeries around these days, so be sure to get good sourdough for this sandwich. The texture works really well with the beef.

2 slices of sourdough bread
olive oil
sea salt
2 tomatoes
small pot of pesto
rare roast beef, sliced as
    thinly as possible
1 bag of rocket leaves
salt and freshly ground
    black pepper

SERVES 1

BRUSH THE SOURDOUGH WITH OLIVE OIL, sprinkle with sea salt and grill on both sides. Cut the tomatoes in half and grill them.

SPREAD THE SOURDOUGH WITH PESTO, add some slices of beef and top with rocket leaves and grilled tomatoes. Season with salt and pepper to taste.

PROSCIUTTO WITH FIGS AND BALSAMIC

This is a variation on the classic Parma ham and melon dish.
You can use nectarines instead of figs if you prefer.

12 very thin slices of
    prosciutto
8 ripe figs, skin on
1 bag of rocket leaves
Parmesan cheese shavings
2 tbsp balsamic vinegar

SERVES 4

LAYER THE SLICES OF PROSCIUTTO on a serving dish.

CUT THE FIGS INTO QUARTERS and arrange them on the dish, then add a few rocket leaves and Parmesan shavings.

DRIZZLE WITH BALSAMIC VINEGAR and serve immediately.

CROSTINI

These tasty morsels make an ideal starter for a summer dinner party.
Be warned – it's all too easy to eat more of these than you should!

4 slices of sourdough bread
olive oil
garlic
rock salt

*For the broad bean, pea
and goats' cheese topping*
100g cooked peas
100g cooked broad beans
50g goats' cheese, crumbled
1 tsp chopped mint
salt and freshly ground
    black pepper

For the tomato topping
2 tomatoes, diced
2 tbsp olive oil
1 tbsp vinegar
handful of basil leaves, torn
salt and freshly ground
    black pepper

*For the Gorgonzola
and walnut topping*
100g Gorgonzola cheese
10 walnuts, crushed
dash of olive oil
salt and freshly ground
    black pepper

For the chicken liver topping
2 tbsp olive oil
1 garlic clove, crushed
1 shallot, finely chopped
250g organic chicken livers
1 tbsp brandy
2 tbsp cream (optional)
salt and freshly ground
    black pepper

SERVES 4

DRIZZLE OLIVE OIL over the slices of sourdough, rub with a cut clove of garlic and season with rock salt.

HEAT A GRIDDLE and grill the bread on both sides. Add whichever topping you choose.

Broad bean, pea and goats' cheese crostini

MIX ALL THE INGREDIENTS IN A BOWL and season well. Put on top of the grilled sourdough.

Tomato crostini

DRESS THE TOMATOES with the oil and vinegar and season well. Add the basil and divide between the slices of sourdough.

Gorgonzola and walnut crostini

MASH THE GORGONZOLA slightly and add a touch of olive oil. Season, then spread the mixture onto the toasted sourdough. Finish with a sprinkling of crushed walnuts.

Chicken liver crostini (not shown)

TRIM THE CHICKEN LIVERS and remove any sinew.

HEAT THE OIL IN A PAN. Add the crushed garlic and shallot and sauté until soft. Add the chicken livers and sauté briefly until just cooked, then add the brandy.

TRANSFER TO A FOOD PROCESSOR and blitz to a smooth purée. Season and add the cream, if using. Place on the toasted sourdough and finish with a dash of olive oil.

CARROT AND COURGETTE FRITTERS

These are easy to do and make a perfect vegetarian starter. You can prepare the mixture in advance and fry the fritters when you're ready to eat.

4 small courgettes, grated
3 small carrots, grated
3 eggs
4 spring onions, chopped
2 tbsp chopped flatleaf
   parsley
2 tbsp coriander
2 pinches of paprika or
   chilli powder
225g plain flour
groundnut oil, for
   deep-frying
squeeze of fresh lemon juice
salt and freshly ground
   black pepper

SERVES 4

PUT THE GRATED VEGETABLES into a bowl and add the eggs, spring onions, herbs, spices and seasoning. Mix well, then add the flour and work everything together. Form the mixture into balls about the size of golf balls.

HEAT THE GROUNDNUT OIL in a large pan until a piece of bread sizzles when dropped into it. Drop in a few fritters at a time and fry until golden. Drain the fritters on kitchen paper and serve with a squeeze of lemon.

NEW POTATO CRISPS WITH BLACK PEPPER AND PARMESAN

2 tbsp groundnut oil
6 large Charlotte potatoes,
   very finely sliced
handful of freshly grated
   Parmesan cheese
salt and freshly ground
   black pepper

SERVES 4

HEAT THE OIL in a heavy-based pan and add a single layer of potato slices – don't overcrowd the pan. Fry until golden, turning once.

REMOVE AND SEASON with salt, pepper and grated Parmesan. Continue until all the potatoes are cooked.

PIZZA

I've suggested some ideas for pizza toppings here, but experiment to your heart's content. The important thing is to keep all the filling ingredients in small pieces and spread them evenly over the pizza. That way you get a little bit of everything in every mouthful.

670ml lukewarm water
1 tsp sugar
18g fresh yeast or 2 sachets of dried
1kg strong white flour
15g salt

Toppings
Tomato sauce (see page 282)
chopped ham
finely sliced mushrooms
chopped olives
anchovies
sliced mozzarella
chopped garlic

MAKES 4–6 PIZZAS

POUR ABOUT 100ML of the lukewarm water into a jug and add the sugar and yeast. Stir and leave in a warm place for 10 minutes.

IF YOU HAVE A KITCHENAID, put the flour and salt in the bowl, add the yeast and the rest of the water and mix with the dough hook. Transfer to a bowl large enough to hold the dough when it has risen and leave for about 2 hours in a warm place, until doubled in size.

OTHERWISE, MIX THE FLOUR WITH THE SALT in a large bowl, make a well in the middle and add the yeast mixture and the rest of the water. Knead to a dough and leave to rise as above.

WHEN THE DOUGH HAS DOUBLED IN SIZE, divide it into 4–6 pieces, depending on how big you want your pizzas. You can roll the dough out with a rolling pin or, if you want to try being a bit flash, pull it out with your hands like they do in your local pizza parlour. Try spinning your pizza dough, too!

PREHEAT THE OVEN to 220°C/Fan 200°C/Gas mark 7. Lightly grease some baking sheets with olive oil and place the pizza bases on the sheets.

SPREAD SOME TOMATO SAUCE over the pizzas, making it as thin or thick as you like. Add chopped ham, mushrooms, olives, anchovies, mozzarella, garlic – whatever you want – and spread evenly over the pizza base.

COOK THE PIZZAS for 5–8 minutes, until the base is crisp and the top is beginning to bubble. If your pizzas are quite thick, turn the oven down to 190°C/Fan 170°C/Gas mark 5 and cook for another 5 minutes.

SAUSAGES WITH LENTILS AND HERBS

A lovely supper dish, this is good served with cavolo nero or spring greens.

150g lentils
1 thyme sprig
1 rosemary sprig
1 tbsp olive oil
1 onion, finely sliced
4 Lyonnaise sausages
50g chopped pancetta
   (optional)
1 tbsp chopped flatleaf
   parsley
salt and freshly ground
   black pepper

SERVES 4

PUT THE LENTILS IN A PAN and pour in cold water to cover. Add the thyme and rosemary and bring to the boil. Simmer until the lentils are cooked.

MEANWHILE, HEAT THE OLIVE OIL in a pan and sauté the onion until softened. Remove the onion and set aside, then sauté the sausages with the chopped pancetta. Put the onion back in the pan.

ADD THE COOKED LENTILS to the sausages and pancetta, pour in 100ml of water, then simmer until you have a thick sauce. Season and finish with chopped parsley.

SOUPS

CELERIAC, APPLE AND CHESTNUT SOUP

50g butter
2 tbsp olive oil
1 head of celeriac,
   peeled and chopped
2 thyme sprigs
2 small onions, chopped
1 litre Chicken or Vegetable
   stock (see pages 282–283)
4 Granny Smith apples,
   diced
6 vacuum-packed chestnuts,
   grated
salt and freshly ground
   black pepper

SERVES 4

HEAT THE BUTTER AND OLIVE OIL in a pan, then add the celeriac, thyme and onion and sauté lightly.

POUR IN THE STOCK, season and cover the pan with a lid or a circle of baking parchment. Simmer until the celeriac is just done.

ADD THE DICED APPLES to the soup and cook for 5 minutes more. Remove the thyme sprigs, pour the soup into a blender and blitz until smooth. Check the seasoning and serve with a sprinkling of grated chestnuts.

LEEK AND POTATO SOUP

50g butter
4 leeks, washed and sliced
1 small onion, chopped
5 medium potatoes,
   cut into chunks
1 litre Chicken stock
   (see page 282)
500ml double cream
1 tbsp chopped chives
salt and freshly ground
   black pepper

SERVES 4

MELT THE BUTTER in a large pan, add the leeks and onion and sauté until soft. Add the potatoes and cook for a few minutes.

POUR IN THE CHICKEN STOCK and cook until the potatoes are soft. Pour the soup into a blender and blitz until smooth, then tip back into the pan.

SEASON TO TASTE and add cream until you have the consistency you like. Warm through again before serving or chill in the fridge and serve cold. Garnish with chopped chives.

WATERCRESS SOUP

100g butter
1 onion, chopped
1 garlic clove, chopped
500g potatoes, diced
grating of nutmeg
1 litre Chicken or Vegetable
    stock (see pages 282–283)
4 bunches of watercress,
    stalks removed
4 tbsp crème fraîche
salt and freshly ground
    black pepper

SERVES 4

MELT THE BUTTER in a pan, add the onion, garlic and potatoes and cook until soft. Add the nutmeg and seasoning, then pour in the stock and bring to the boil.

ADD THE WATERCRESS and cook for 30 seconds, then transfer the soup to a blender or food processor and blitz until smooth. Serve right away if the soup is smooth enough and you want to eat it hot.

TO SERVE COLD, pass the soup through a sieve into a bowl set over ice. Don't miss out this stage as it helps chill the soup quickly so it keeps its lovely bright green colour. Continue chilling in the fridge.

ADD A SPOONFUL of crème fraîche to each bowl when serving, hot or cold.

WALNUT SOUP

175g shelled walnuts, plus
    extra 50g for garnish
1 large garlic clove, peeled
1 litre Chicken or Vegetable
    stock (see pages 282–283)
150ml single cream
drizzle of olive oil
1 tbsp chopped chives
salt and freshly ground
    black pepper

SERVES 4

PUT THE 175G OF WALNUTS AND GARLIC into a food processor and purée until you have a thick paste. Add a touch of stock to loosen the purée.

ADD THE REST OF THE STOCK, a little at a time, and the cream, then blend until you have a smooth soup.

POUR THE SOUP INTO A PAN, season to taste and heat gently before serving. Serve with a drizzle of olive oil and a garnish with a few chopped walnuts and chives.

ONION SOUP WITH CHEESE TOASTS

You can buy good beef stock now, so this great winter warmer is easy to make.

1 tbsp olive oil
4 large onions, thinly sliced
2 garlic cloves, sliced
150ml red wine
dash of brandy
dash of Worcestershire
   sauce
700ml beef stock
50g Parmesan cheese,
   freshly grated
50g Gruyère, freshly grated
1 French stick, cut into slices
1 tbsp chopped flatleaf
   parsley
salt and freshly ground
   black pepper

SERVES 4

HEAT THE OIL in a large saucepan and add the onions and garlic. Cook until soft and nicely caramelised and coloured.

POUR IN THE RED WINE, brandy and Worcestershire sauce and stir with a wooden spoon, scraping up any sticky bits from the bottom of the pan.

ADD THE STOCK and cook for 15 minutes until you have a lovely thick soup. Check the seasoning, bearing in mind you will be adding salty cheese when serving the soup.

PILE THE GRATED CHEESE onto the slices of bread and place under a hot grill until the cheese is bubbling.

GARNISH THE SOUP with chopped parsley and serve with the cheese toasts on top.

CHICKEN NOODLE SOUP

I love going to Chinese restaurants and this heart-warming soup
is one of my favourite dishes. This is my version.

2 tbsp olive oil
2 spring onions, chopped
1 heaped tsp chopped
    root ginger
1 garlic clove, chopped
½ tsp chopped chilli
900ml Chicken stock
    (see page 282)
2 chicken legs, skinned
6 chestnut mushrooms,
    sliced
4 baby sweetcorn, sliced
100g baby spinach
2 heads of pak choi, sliced
250g precooked noodles
1 tsp chopped mint
1 tsp chopped coriander
salt and freshly ground
    black pepper

SERVES 4

HEAT THE OLIVE OIL in a large pan. Add the chopped spring
onions, ginger, garlic and chilli and cook gently for 5 minutes.

POUR IN THE STOCK and add the chicken legs and simmer
until the chicken is cooked.

REMOVE THE CHICKEN LEGS, shred the meat and put it back into
the soup. Add the mushrooms, baby corn, spinach and pak choi,
then season and bring back to the boil. Add the noodles and herbs
and cook just long enough to warm the noodles through. Check
the seasoning and serve.

CHICKPEA SOUP WITH MINT AND GARLIC

2 x 400g cans of chickpeas
50ml olive oil
2 large garlic cloves,
    chopped
1 litre Vegetable stock
    (see page 283)
juice of 1 lemon
1 tsp chopped mint
1 tsp chopped flatleaf parley
salt and freshly ground
    black pepper

SERVES 4

DRAIN THE CHICKPEAS, reserving the juice. Heat a little of the olive oil in a saucepan and sauté the garlic, then add the chickpeas. Pour in the stock and bring it to the boil.

POUR THE SOUP INTO A BLENDER and blitz to a purée, then put it back into the pan. Add the reserved juice from the chickpeas and check the soup is the consistency you like. Add more liquid if necessary.

WARM THE SOUP THROUGH, then add the rest of the olive oil and the lemon juice. Season to taste. Add the chopped herbs just before serving.

CHILLED CUCUMBER SOUP

4 cucumbers
½ bunch of tarragon
½ tbsp grated horseradish
4 tsp horseradish relish
2 shallots, chopped
400ml Vegetable stock
    (see page 283)
500ml yoghurt
salt and freshly ground
    black pepper

SERVES 4

PEEL 2 OF THE CUCUMBERS and remove the seeds from all of them. Set aside half a peeled cucumber for the garnish, then slice the rest and place the slices in a large bowl.

REMOVE THE LEAVES FROM THE TARRAGON and set aside, then add the stalks to the cucumber. Add the grated horseradish and relish, shallots, stock and yoghurt. Season to taste and leave to marinate overnight.

NEXT DAY, remove the tarragon stalks and blitz the soup in a blender. Pass the soup through a sieve, then put it back in the fridge to chill.

DICE the remaining half cucumber. Serve the chilled soup garnished with diced cucumber and tarragon leaves. Smoked salmon on toast goes well with this soup.

PRAWN AND ALMOND SOUP

Thickening soup with almonds is a Spanish touch and
the nuts work surprisingly well with prawns.

2 tbsp olive oil
1 small onion, finely
    chopped
50g diced potato
1 tsp thyme leaves,
    picked from stems
50g freshly ground almonds
500ml Chicken or Fish stock
    (see pages 282–283)
150g shelled and diced
    prawns
handful of spinach
1 tbsp chopped coriander
salt and freshly ground
    black pepper

SERVES 4

HEAT THE OLIVE OIL in a pan and sauté the onion until soft.
Add the diced potato and thyme leaves. Add the ground almonds
and cook for 30 seconds.

POUR IN THE STOCK, bring to the boil and simmer until the
potato is cooked.

ADD THE PRAWNS and spinach and cook for a couple of minutes.
Season and serve garnished with chopped coriander.

TOMATO AND BREAD SOUP

Only make this when tomatoes are in season and at their best.

12 over-ripe tomatoes
60ml olive oil
1 small red onion,
    finely chopped
1 garlic clove, crushed
4 slices of good firm
    Italian-style bread
handful of fresh basil leaves
salt and freshly ground
    black pepper

SERVES 4

SLICE THE TOMATOES, removing the cores, and put them
in a large bowl with the olive oil, onion and garlic.

ADD THE BREAD, torn into pieces, then pour over 500ml
of water. Leave to soak overnight.

NEXT DAY, blend the soup, then season and serve garnished
with fresh basil leaves.

PEA SOUP

You can use frozen peas for this beautiful soup, so it is really quick and simple to make (see picture opposite).

1 litre Vegetable stock
    (see page 283)
500g frozen peas
6 mint leaves
200ml crème fraîche
drizzle of olive oil,
    for serving
salt and freshly ground
    black pepper

SERVES 4

POUR THE VEGETABLE STOCK into a pan and bring to the boil – you can use water if you don't have any veg stock.

ADD THE FROZEN PEAS and mint leaves, bring back to the boil and cook for 2 minutes. Drain, reserving the stock.

BLITZ THE PEAS in a food processor or blender with half the stock. Pour the purée back into the pan and add enough of the remaining stock to make a smooth soup. Season to taste.

ADD THE CRÈME FRAÎCHE and a drizzle of olive oil before serving.

SUMMER MINESTRONE

2 tbsp olive oil
1 celery stick, diced
1 onion, chopped finely
1 garlic clove, chopped
750ml Vegetable stock
    (see page 283)
200g shelled peas
200g shelled broad beans
1 courgette, diced
1 fennel bulb, diced
6 mint leaves
handful of basil leaves
1 tsp chopped tarragon
1 baby gem lettuce,
    shredded
salt and freshly ground
    black pepper

SERVES 4

HEAT 1 TABLESPOON OF OLIVE OIL in a pan and sauté the celery, onion and garlic. Cover with vegetable stock and cook for about 10 minutes.

ADD THE REST OF THE VEGETABLES, season, and bring back to the boil. Simmer for 5 minutes.

TO FINISH THE SOUP, add the herbs and baby gem lettuce, check the seasoning and add a dash of olive oil.

CLAM AND TOMATO SOUP

This is inspired by shellfish soups I've eaten in Spain and southern Italy. Use good-quality passata – easy to find now – for a gutsy Mediterranean flavour.

2 tbsp olive oil
4 garlic cloves, finely
 chopped
1 shallot, chopped
500g clams, well scrubbed
250ml white wine
1 tsp chopped thyme
2 fennel bulbs
1 onion, diced
1 tsp seeded and chopped
 red chilli
100g tomato passata
4 slices of sourdough bread
1 tbsp chopped flatleaf
 parsley
1 tbsp chopped basil
salt and freshly ground
 black pepper

SERVES 4

HEAT THE OLIVE OIL in a large pan and lightly sauté the garlic and shallot. Add the clams, white wine and thyme, put a lid on the pan and cook until the clams open.

DRAIN THE CLAMS, discarding any that haven't opened, and reserve the juices. Remove half the clams from the shells and leave the rest as they are. Set the clams and juice aside.

REMOVE THE OUTER LEAVES and core from the fennel and dice the rest. Add the diced fennel and onion to the pan with the chilli and sauté until soft.

ADD THE CLAMS and the tomato passata. Strain the reserved clam juice and add it to the pan, then bring to the boil. Check the seasoning and if necessary add a touch of water.

TOAST THE SOURDOUGH and place a slice in each bowl. Serve the soup on top and garnish with parsley and basil.

RIBOLLITA

You'll see this classic soup on the menus of all the good
trattorias in Tuscany. It looks like a long list of ingredients
but it's easy to make, so don't be put off.

1 tbsp olive oil
2 small red onions,
    roughly chopped
2 carrots, roughly chopped
3 celery sticks, trimmed
    and chopped
3 garlic cloves, chopped
pinch of ground fennel
    seeds
pinch of dried red chilli
1 bay leaf
500ml Vegetable or Chicken
    stock (see pages 282–283)
1 small potato, chopped
1 x 400g can of cannellini
    beans, drained
1 x 400g can of good-quality
    plum tomatoes
1 tomato, squashed
310g cavolo nero, leaves
    and stalks finely sliced
2 large handfuls of good-
    quality stale bread,
    torn into chunks
drizzle of extra virgin olive
    oil, the best you can find,
    for serving
sea salt and freshly ground
    black pepper

SERVES 4

HEAT THE OLIVE OIL in a large pan and sauté the onions, carrots,
celery and garlic. Add the fennel seeds, chilli and bay leaf, then
pour in the stock. Add the potato and bring to a simmer and cook
until the vegetables are just done.

ADD THE BEANS, canned tomatoes, fresh tomato and cavolo nero
and bring back to the boil. Check the seasoning.

PUT SOME TORN BREAD into the bottom of each bowl, pour in the
soup and drizzle with a little extra virgin olive oil before serving.

LAMB BROTH

Colin Buchan, head chef at the York and Albany in London, makes this soup – a sign of his Scottish roots, perhaps? It's one of my favourites.

2 tbsp olive oil
1 whole carrot
½ onion
1 garlic clove, crushed
1 celery stick, cut in half
5 black peppercorns
1 thyme sprig
1 rosemary sprig
2 lamb necks
3 litres Chicken stock
    (see page 282)
1 carrot, diced
1 onion, finely chopped
1 leek, finely chopped
100g pearl barley
large handful of chopped
    kale or cabbage
1 tbsp chopped tarragon
1 tbsp chopped flatleaf
    parsley
salt and freshly ground
    black pepper

SERVES 8

HEAT A TABLESPOON OF OLIVE OIL in a large heavy-based pan. Add the whole carrot, onion, garlic and celery and sauté briefly. Add the peppercorns and herbs and cook for a minute or two more.

REMOVE THE VEGETABLES FROM THE PAN, add the lamb necks and cook until lightly browned on all sides. Put the vegetables back in the pan and pour in the stock. Season, bring to the boil and simmer for 2 hours.

TAKE THE PAN OFF THE HEAT and strain the stock. Set the stock and lamb aside and discard the vegetables. Wash the pan.

HEAT THE REST OF THE OIL in the clean pan and sauté the diced carrot, onion and leek with the pearl barley. Pour in the reserved stock, cover and simmer until the vegetables are cooked.

SHRED THE MEAT FROM THE LAMB NECKS and add this to the pan. Bring to the boil again, add the kale or cabbage and allow it to wilt. Check the seasoning and finish with chopped tarragon and parsley.

SALADS

GREEN BEAN SALAD WITH HAZELNUTS AND HERBS

Nuts and beans are a great combination. If you want to add a touch
of sweetness, add some raisins or sultanas.

500g French beans
50g butter
50g hazelnuts, skinned
2 shallots, finely sliced
1 tbsp chopped flatleaf
    parsley
1 tbsp chopped tarragon
1 baby gem lettuce,
    shredded
3 tbsp Classic vinaigrette
    (see page 282)
salt and freshly ground
    black pepper

SERVES 4-6

TOP AND TAIL THE BEANS. Bring a pan of salted water to the boil
and cook the beans for 4 minutes. Drain and immediately refresh
in iced water.

HEAT THE BUTTER in a non-stick frying pan until bubbling. Add
the hazelnuts and roast over a medium heat for 2–3 minutes,
constantly shaking the pan to prevent the nuts sticking. Remove
and leave to cool, then chop roughly.

MIX THE CHOPPED NUTS with the beans, shallots, herbs and
lettuce in a bowl. Add the vinaigrette and season.

CAULIFLOWER, RAISIN AND CUMIN SALAD

The secret is to dress the cauliflower while warm so it absorbs the flavours.

1 cauliflower
3 tbsp Classic vinaigrette
    (see page 282)
½ tsp ground cumin
3 tbsp golden raisins
50g chopped walnuts
2 tbsp chopped coriander
salt and freshly ground
    black pepper

SERVES 4

BREAK THE CAULIFLOWER into small bite-sized florets. Bring
a pan of salted water to the boil and cook the cauliflower until
just tender, then drain.

ADD ENOUGH VINAIGRETTE to coat the warm cauliflower. Add
the cumin, then the raisins and walnuts and check the seasoning.
Garnish with the chopped coriander and serve at room temperature.

RED CABBAGE, APPLE AND PARSLEY SALAD

Ideally, marinate the cabbage overnight for the best flavour.

1 red cabbage
3 tbsp honey
125ml red wine vinegar
100g raisins
50ml balsamic vinegar
4 eating apples
    (Cox or Braeburn)
100ml olive oil
2 tbsp chopped flatleaf
    parsley
salt and freshly ground
    black pepper

SERVES 4

REMOVE THE OUTER LEAVES from the red cabbage, then cut it in half and remove the core. Finely shred the cabbage and place it in a bowl.

PUT THE HONEY and red wine vinegar in a pan and heat until the honey has melted. Pour this mixture over the cabbage, then cover and leave to marinate for at least 4–5 hours.

NEXT DAY, PUT THE RAISINS in a bowl with the balsamic vinegar and leave to soak for 10 minutes.

JUST BEFORE SERVING, slice the apples and add them to the marinated cabbage, with the olive oil, parsley, soaked raisins and balsamic. Season with salt and pepper to taste.

BROCCOLI, FETA AND CHERRY TOMATO SALAD

400g broccoli, split into
    bite-sized florets
100g feta cheese, diced
500g cherry tomatoes,
    halved
3 tbsp Classic vinaigrette
    (see page 282)
freshly ground black pepper

SERVES 4

BRING A PAN OF SALTED WATER to the boil and cook the broccoli until tender but not mushy. Drain and immediately refresh in some iced water.

PUT THE BROCCOLI in a serving bowl with the feta cheese and cherry tomatoes.

GENTLY TOSS WITH THE DRESSING and season with pepper. You shouldn't need salt, since the feta is usually salty enough.

BUTTERBEAN, SMOKED BACON AND GARLIC SALAD

Beans and bacon are a great combination. Smoked bacon is best for this salad.

1 x 400g can of butterbeans
2 tbsp olive oil
1 garlic clove, crushed
110g smoked bacon, cut into
    small strips (lardons)
zest of 1 lemon
8 tbsp olive oil
2 tbsp chopped flatleaf
    parsley
salt and freshly ground
    black pepper

SERVES 2–3

DRAIN THE BEANS and rinse them under cold water.

HEAT THE OIL in a pan and sauté the garlic – don't let it colour. Add the bacon and fry until crisp.

PUT THE BEANS in a bowl and add the garlic, bacon and remaining ingredients. Season and serve.

ROCKET, FETA AND BREAD SALAD

Feata has a lovely texture and salty taste which really works here, but grilled haloumi is a good alternative for a change.

200g rocket leaves
1 tbsp chopped mint
250g feta cheese, diced
2 tbsp olive oil
1 garlic clove, crushed
1 rosemary sprig
250g sourdough bread or
    focaccia, cut into cubes
100ml Red wine vinaigrette
    (see page 282)
salt and freshly ground
    black pepper

SERVES 4

MIX THE ROCKET, mint and feta in a salad bowl.

HEAT THE OLIVE OIL in a frying pan, add the garlic and rosemary, then fry the cubes of bread until crispy.

ADD THE FRIED BREAD to the salad and toss with enough vinaigrette to coat everything lightly. Season and serve immediately.

GARLIC-ROASTED NEW POTATO SALAD

500g small new potatoes,
    quartered
2 tbsp olive oil
1 tbsp chopped rosemary
4 garlic cloves, finely
    chopped
2 tsp salt
1 tsp coarsely ground
    black pepper
2 heaped tbsp good
    mayonnaise
3 tbsp finely chopped parsley
juice of 1 lemon

SERVES 4-6

PREHEAT THE OVEN to 200°C/Fan 180°C/Gas mark 6. In a bowl, toss the potatoes with the olive oil, rosemary, garlic, salt and pepper.

PUT THE POTATOES in a roasting tin in a single layer with the skin sides facing down. Roast for about 45 minutes, shaking twice during this time. Carefully transfer the cooked potatoes to a bowl, being careful not to break them up, and leave to cool to room temperature.

MIX THE MAYONNAISE with the parsley and lemon juice and add to the potatoes. Stir gently so the potatoes are well coated, then serve.

PRAWN, MANGO AND FENNEL SALAD

The sweetness of the mango works perfectly with the prawns in this salad.

2 tbsp olive oil
pinch of dried chilli
300g raw prawns, peeled
    and deveined
1 fennel bulb, finely sliced
3–4 tbsp Classic vinaigrette
    (see page 282)
1 tbsp chopped parsley
1 tsp chopped coriander
1 mango, peeled and sliced
salt and freshly ground
    black pepper

SERVES 4

HEAT THE OLIVE OIL in a frying pan. Add the chilli, then the prawns and sauté the prawns until cooked and pink. Remove from the pan and allow to cool slightly.

MIX THE FENNEL with the vinaigrette and herbs, then season with salt and pepper.

PLACE THE FENNEL AND SLICED MANGO in a serving dish, then add the cooked prawns on top. Serve immediately.

GRILLED VEGETABLES AND COUSCOUS SALAD

Don't be tempted to skip skinning the peppers – it does make a difference. Serve this salad at room temperature, not fridge cold, to taste all the flavours at their best.

4 red peppers
2 courgettes, cut into
    thin diagonal slices
1 aubergine, cut into
    thin rounds
1 fennel bulb, thinly sliced
2 tbsp olive oil
250g couscous
Classic vinaigrette
    (see page 282)
1 bunch of basil, chopped
    at the last minute
salt and freshly ground
    black pepper

SERVES 4-6

FIRST SKIN THE PEPPERS. Put them in a hot oven until the skins are black, then place them in a bowl and cover with cling film. When cool enough to handle, peel off the blackened skin. Alternatively, you can blacken the peppers over an open flame.

PUT THE COURGETTE, AUBERGINE AND FENNEL SLICES in a bowl and add the olive oil. Toss until all the vegetables are coated, then season to taste.

HEAT A RIDGED GRILL PAN and grill the vegetable slices on both sides. When they are done, put them back in the bowl and cover with cling film so they steam and carry on cooking.

COOK THE COUSCOUS according to the instructions on the packet, then mix it with the vegetables in a serving bowl.

ADD THE VINAIGRETTE, being careful not to saturate the salad, then the basil. Check the seasoning and serve.

SPICED CHICKPEA SALAD

This salad tastes best the day after making, when the flavours
have had a chance to mingle and develop.

1 onion, finely chopped
4 tbsp olive oil, plus more
   to dress, if needed
3cm piece of root ginger,
   grated
1 red chilli, seeded
   and finely chopped
2 tsp curry powder
1 tsp ground cumin
1 tsp ground coriander
pinch of turmeric
1 garlic clove, chopped
2 x 400g cans of chickpeas
1 tbsp chopped coriander
1 tbsp chopped chives
1 tbsp chopped flatleaf
   parsley
salt and freshly ground
   black pepper

SERVES 4–6

GENTLY SAUTÉ THE ONION in olive oil for 10 minutes without
allowing it to colour. Add the ginger, chilli, spices and garlic
and cook for 2 minutes longer.

DRAIN THE CHICKPEAS and rinse them under cold water, then
add them to the warm onions. Allow to cool to room temperature,
then add the chopped herbs.

SEASON THE SALAD before serving and drizzle over a little more
olive oil, if needed.

CHICKEN AND CHICKPEA SALAD

I made this one night when I had some leftover roast chicken in the fridge and nothing planned for supper. I added some canned chickpeas and frozen peas – both of which I always have handy – and mixed everything together to make a nice little salad. Quick, easy and delicious.

300g cooked chicken
100g cooked green peas
100g canned chickpeas
1 tbsp chopped parsley
½ tbsp chopped mint
100g rocket leaves
4 tbsp Classic
   vinaigrette (see page 282)
crumbled goats' cheese or
   ricotta
salt and freshly ground
   black pepper

SERVES 2

SHRED THE CHICKEN, including any crispy skin, and place it in a large serving bowl.

ADD THE PEAS, DRAINED CHICKPEAS, herbs and rocket. Season, add the vinaigrette and mix everything together well. Add the crumbled cheese and serve.

PUY LENTILS, SPINACH AND GOATS' CURD SALAD

250g Puy lentils
2 celery sticks, sliced
1 bunch of spring onions, chopped
1 tbsp chopped tarragon
2 handfuls of baby spinach, washed and drained
3–4 tbsp Classic vinaigrette (see page 282)
100g goats' curd (or soft goats' cheese)
salt and freshly ground black pepper

SERVES 4

PUT THE PUY LENTILS in a pan and cover with cold water. Bring to the boil, then turn the heat down and simmer until soft – about 30 minutes.

DRAIN THE LENTILS and put them in a bowl. Add the celery and spring onions and mix well. Stir in the tarragon and baby spinach – the leaves will wilt in the heat of the lentils – then add the vinaigrette and season.

SPOON ON THE GOATS' CURD just before serving.

PEAR, CHICORY AND BLUE CHEESE SALAD

This is a good way of using pears that are not perfectly ripe.
You can use ripe pears, but be careful not to overcook them.

grated zest of ½ lemon
juice of 1 lemon
250g granulated sugar
4 pears
2 large heads of chicory
1 tbsp chopped flatleaf parsley
3 tbsp Classic vinaigrette (see page 282)
100g blue cheese, crumbled
salt and freshly ground black pepper

SERVES 4-6

PUT THE LEMON ZEST AND JUICE in a pan large enough to hold all the pears and add the sugar and some water. Bring to the boil so the sugar dissolves, then add the pears. Top up with more boiling water if necessary and put a plate on top of the pears to keep them submerged.

SIMMER THE PEARS until cooked and a knife goes through them easily. Leave to cool.

SLICE THE PEARS and cut the chicory into strips. Mix them with the parsley and vinaigrette in a serving bowl and add the blue cheese. Season to taste and serve.

NEW POTATO AND MACKEREL SALAD WITH MUSTARD DRESSING

Be sure to dress the potatoes while still warm so they absorb
the vinegar and serve the salad at room temperature.

12 small new potatoes
Classic vinaigrette
   (see page 282)
2 tsp Dijon mustard
 2 smoked mackerel fillets
2 tbsp chopped flatleaf
   parsley
1 bunch of watercress
1 bunch of spring onions,
   chopped
salt and freshly ground
   black pepper

SERVES 4

PUT THE POTATOES in a pan of cold salted water and bring to the
boil. Reduce the heat and simmer for about 10 minutes, or until
the potatoes are soft when pierced with the tip of a knife. Drain the
potatoes, slice them and dress with the vinaigrette and mustard.

SHRED THE MACKEREL FILLETS and mix with the potatoes, then
add the parsley, watercress and chopped spring onions. Be gentle,
as you don't want the salad to get mushy. Season and serve.

MUSHROOM, OLIVE AND MINT SALAD

Feel free to use whatever mushrooms you can find. I love this made with ceps.

250g wild mushrooms
2 tbsp olive oil
1 garlic clove, crushed
1 baby gem lettuce
1 bag of rocket leaves
50g green olives, sliced
2 tbsp chopped mint
salt and freshly ground
   black pepper

SERVES 4

WIPE THE MUSHROOMS or wash them gently if very dirty,
then trim and slice them.

HEAT THE OLIVE OIL in a pan. Add the crushed garlic and wild
mushrooms and sauté until the mushrooms are tender but not
soggy. Season with salt and pepper.

SEPARATE THE LETTUCE LEAVES and put them in a bowl with
the rocket. Add the olives and mint, then top with the sautéed
mushrooms. Serve immediately.

MACKEREL, APPLE, CELERY AND RADISH SALAD

Mackerel is cheap and delicious – a very underrated fish in my opinion and I'd like to see it used much more. This crunchy salad is a good match to the the rich flavour of the fish.

2 tsp coarse grain mustard
1 tbsp chopped chives
Classic vinaigrette
  (see page 282)
2 fresh mackerel, filleted
olive oil, for greasing the
  baking sheet
3 celery sticks, peeled
  and sliced
2 apples, washed, cored
  and sliced
8 breakfast radishes, sliced
½ bunch of watercress
1 lemon, cut into wedges,
  for serving
salt and freshly ground
  black pepper

SERVES 4

MIX THE MUSTARD and chives into the vinaigrette, season and set aside.

PLACE THE MACKEREL FILLETS, skin-side up, on an oiled baking sheet. Place under a hot grill and cook until the flesh is done and the skin is beginning to bubble – 4–5 minutes. Turn the fillets if necessary.

MIX THE CELERY, APPLE, RADISHES and watercress with the mustard vinaigrette. Place the salad in a serving dish and add the mackerel fillets with their cooking juices. Check the seasoning and serve with some lemon wedges.

SWEET POTATO, CHORIZO AND RED PEPPER SALAD

2 sweet potatoes, diced
    with skin on
2 tbsp olive oil
pinch of ground cumin
pinch of cayenne
100g chorizo, diced
2 red peppers, skinned
    (see page 52) and cut
    into strips
2 tbsp chopped coriander
4 tbsp Red wine vinaigrette
    (see page 282)
salt and freshly ground
    black pepper

SERVES 4

PREHEAT THE OVEN to 180°C/Fan 160°C/Gas mark 4. Toss the sweet potatoes with a tablespoon of oil and the spices and transfer to a baking sheet. Cook in the oven for about 30 minutes, turning occasionally.

HEAT THE REST OF THE OIL in a frying pan and fry the diced chorizo until cooked.

MIX THE CHORIZO with cooked sweet potatoes, red peppers and coriander and gently stir in the vinaigrette. Check the seasoning and serve.

CHICKPEA AND ROSEMARY SALAD

This salad goes well with lamb or chicken dishes
or can be served on its own as a light lunch.

2 x 400g cans of chickpeas
1 jar of piquillo peppers
1 red onion, diced
handful of celery leaves,
    chopped
3–4 tbsp Red wine
    vinaigrette (see page 282)
½ tsp crushed chilli flakes
½ tsp chopped rosemary
salt and freshly ground
    black pepper

SERVES 4

DRAIN AND RINSE THE CHICKPEAS and put them in a bowl. Slice the peppers and add them to the chickpeas with the diced onion and chopped celery leaves.

ADD THE VINAIGRETTE and chilli flakes and season to taste.

DRESS THE SALAD and toss well, then add the chopped rosemary before serving.

CHICKEN AND GOATS' CHEESE SALAD WITH GREMOLATA

200g green beans
2 spring onions, chopped
300g cooked chicken, shredded
100g goats' cheese, crumbled

For the gremolata
grated zest of 1 lemon
75ml olive oil
2 tbsp chopped curly parsley
salt and freshly ground black pepper

SERVES 4

COOK THE GREEN BEANS in a pan of salted boiling water for 4 minutes. Refresh quickly in cold water, then drain.

WHISK THE INGREDIENTS for the gremolata together.

MIX THE BEANS with the spring onions, chicken and goats' cheese, then add the gremolata. Toss well, check the seasoning and serve.

LAMB, BABY GEM AND GOATS' CHEESE SALAD

I got the idea for this salad in Australia when I was served roast leg of lamb with goats' cheese and discovered that they worked well together.

300g roast leg of lamb
1 baby gem lettuce
1 tbsp finely chopped mint
1 tbsp finely chopped basil
75g goats' cheese, crumbled
Classic vinaigrette (see page 282)
salt and freshly ground black pepper

SERVES 4

SLICE THE LAMB into strips. Wash the lettuce and cut it into strips.

MIX THE LAMB, LETTUCE, HERBS AND CHEESE in a serving bowl and add enough vinaigrette to lightly coat all the ingredients. Check the seasoning and serve immediately.

MOROCCAN COUSCOUS SALAD

200g couscous
1 red pepper
1 green pepper
2 celery sticks, thinly sliced
2 tsp ground coriander
1 tsp ground cumin
½ tsp chilli powder
100g raisins
120ml olive oil
4 tbsp white wine vinegar
2 tbsp finely chopped
    coriander
2 tbsp finely chopped
    flatleaf parsley
salt and freshly ground
    black pepper

SERVES 4

COOK THE COUSCOUS according to the instructions on the packet, then leave to cool.

DESEED, CORE AND DICE the peppers and add them to the bowl of couscous, along with the celery.

MIX THE GROUND SPICES, raisins and oil in a frying pan and warm gently over a moderate heat for 3 minutes. Stir in the vinegar and pour this mixture over the couscous.

ADD THE HERBS to the couscous, season with salt and pepper and mix well.

BEEF SALAD

1 tbsp olive oil
1 garlic clove, crushed
1 tsp finely chopped ginger
300g beef fillet, cut
    into strips
8 tbsp soy sauce
juice of ½ lime
½ tbsp chopped tarragon
½ tbsp chopped parsley
handful of mixed salad
    leaves
1 tsp sesame seeds
salt and freshly ground
    black pepper

SERVES 4

HEAT THE OIL in a frying pan, add the garlic and ginger and sauté briefly.

ADD THE BEEF and sear it quickly. Pour in the soy sauce and lime juice and stir with a wooden spoon, scraping up all the sticky bits. Add the tarragon and parsley, then season to taste.

TO FINISH, mix the beef with the salad leaves and sesame seeds. Serve immediately.

ROASTED BUTTERNUT SQUASH, BEETROOT AND SPINACH SALAD

Collect the seeds from the squash, then wash and toast
them and add some to the salad before serving.

1 butternut squash
4 tbsp olive oil, plus extra
    for frying the pancetta
2 rosemary sprigs
2 garlic cloves, crushed
4 cooked beetroot
50g pancetta, chopped
handful of baby spinach
2 tbsp chopped flatleaf
    parsley

*For the sherry vinegar
vinaigrette*
100ml olive oil
10ml sherry vinegar
salt and freshly ground
    black pepper

SERVES 4

PREHEAT THE OVEN to 200°C/Fan 180°C/Gas mark 6.

CUT THE BUTTERNUT SQUASH in half, remove the seeds and
chop the flesh into large chunks.

PUT THE SQUASH in an ovenproof dish with the olive oil, rosemary
and garlic. Roast for about 30 minutes until soft, then remove from
the oven and set aside.

WHISK the vinaigrette ingredients together.

CUT THE COOKED BEETROOT into large chunks and mix it with
the squash in a serving bowl. Sauté the pancetta in a dash of oil
and add it to the beetroot and squash. Add the spinach, parsley
and vinaigrette and toss well – the spinach leaves will wilt in the
heat of the squash. Check the seasoning and serve.

IF YOU PREFER TO BUY RAW BEETROOT and cook it yourself, wash
the beetroot and place it in an ovenproof dish lined with foil. Add
a spoonful of sugar, ½ teaspoon of salt, a dash of sherry or red wine
vinegar and 100ml of water. Scrunch the foil together to make a
parcel and cook the beetroot in a preheated oven – 200°C/Fan
180°C/Gas mark 6 – for about an hour or until soft.

HAM AND GREEN BEAN SALAD WITH MUSTARD DRESSING

Prepare the ham the day before if you can and store it in the fridge with a touch of stock to keep it moist. Freeze the stock to use for soup.

2 ham hocks
1 carrot
1 celery stick
1 small onion
2 garlic cloves
1 thyme sprig
1 rosemary sprig
4 white peppercorns
4 coriander seeds

For the salad
500g green beans,
    topped and tailed
2 tbsp coarse grain mustard
4–6 tbsp Classic vinaigrette
    (see page 282)
salt and freshly ground
    black pepper

SERVES 4-6

PUT THE HAM HOCKS in a large pan, cover with cold water and bring to the boil. Pour the water away, add fresh water and bring back to the boil. Skim off any scum from the surface, then add the vegetables, garlic, herbs, peppercorns and coriander seeds.

BRING BACK TO A SIMMER and cook until the meat falls away from the bones – about 2 hours.

REMOVE THE HAM, discard the vegetables and reserve the stock for use another time. When the ham hocks are cool enough to handle, remove the fat, skin and bones and break the meat into nice large chunks.

COOK THE GREEN BEANS in a pan of salted boiling water for 4 minutes, then drain.

MIX THE BEANS with the cooked meat, mustard and vinaigrette, check the seasoning and serve.

CHICKEN AND BABY SPINACH SALAD

This is a great salad for a party and can be served family-style in a big dish.
Use leftover roast chicken if you prefer.

2 chicken breasts
1 garlic clove, crushed
1 tbsp olive oil
150g green beans
100g baby spinach or green
  salad leaves, washed
1 small head of radicchio
1 tsp chopped flatleaf
  parsley
1 tsp chopped tarragon
1 banana shallot, thinly
  sliced
salt and freshly ground
  black pepper

For the mustard vinaigrette
1 tsp Dijon mustard
100ml olive oil
20ml white wine vinegar

SERVES 4

PREHEAT THE OVEN to 200°C/Fan 180°C/Gas mark 6. Put the chicken breasts, skin-side down, in a roasting tin with the garlic, oil, and 50ml of water. Season with salt and pepper and roast for 10 minutes or until cooked through.

COOK THE GREEN BEANS in a pan of salted boiling water for 4 minutes, then drain.

MAKE THE VINAIGRETTE by mixing the mustard, oil and vinegar, then season to taste.

PUT THE SPINACH OR SALAD LEAVES in a bowl with the radicchio, beans and chopped herbs. Slice the chicken breasts and add them to the salad. Add the sliced shallot and dressing and mix everything together. Check the seasoning, then serve immediately.

LYONNAISE SALAD WITH BLACK PUDDING

The classic French recipe for this dish uses frisée lettuce, but I like mixed salad leaves. The French also add croutons but I prefer to leave these out.

1 tbsp olive oil
4 rashers smoked bacon
100g black pudding, diced
knob of butter
4 eggs
1 bag of mixed salad leaves
1 tsp chopped shallots

For the dressing
4 tbsp olive oil
2 tbsp wine vinegar
1 tsp Dijon mustard
salt and freshly ground
    black pepper

SERVES 4

HEAT THE OLIVE OIL in a frying pan and sauté the bacon and black pudding. Remove and set aside.

WHISK together the ingredients for the dressing.

HEAT THE BUTTER in a pan and fry the eggs.

TOSS THE LEAVES with the black pudding, bacon and shallots and add the dressing. Serve the salad on individual plates, add a fried egg to each serving and season to taste.

PASTA
AND
RISOTTO

SPAGHETTI WITH MUSSELS AND TOMATO SAUCE

This is a favourite summer dish and something you see in every restaurant on Italy's Amalfi coast.

2kg mussels
2 tbsp olive oil
1 thyme sprig
3 garlic cloves, crushed
bunch of flatleaf parsley,
    stalks removed and
    leaves chopped
150ml white wine
350g dried spaghetti
250g Basic tomato sauce
    (see page 282)
pinch of dried chilli
handful of chopped basil
salt and freshly ground
    black pepper

SERVES 4

CLEAN THE MUSSELS under cold running water, scrubbing the shells well and removing the hairy beards. Discard any mussels that are already open.

HEAT A TABLESPOON OF OLIVE OIL in a pan, add the thyme and garlic and the stalks of the parsley. Add the mussels, then pour in the white wine. Cover the pan and cook until the mussels have opened. Discard any that don't open.

REMOVE THE MUSSELS from the pan and reserve the liquid. Take half the mussels out of their shells.

BRING A LARGE PAN OF SALTED WATER to the boil. Add the spaghetti and stir. Cook according to the packet instructions, until the pasta is al dente.

HEAT THE REST OF THE OLIVE OIL in a large pan, add the tomato sauce and dried chilli and warm the sauce through. Check the seasoning.

DRAIN THE SPAGHETTI and put it back in the pan. Toss with the tomato sauce, basil, chopped parsley leaves and shelled mussels. Add the remaining mussels in their shells on top and serve immediately.

SPAGHETTI CARBONARA WITH PEAS

I like to add peas to my summery version of this classic (see picture opposite).

375g dried spaghetti
250g frozen peas, defrosted
2 whole eggs
150ml double cream
50g chopped pancetta
1 tsp olive oil
1 tbsp chopped flatleaf
  parsley
50g Parmesan cheese,
  freshly grated
salt and freshly ground
  black pepper

SERVES 4

BRING A LARGE PAN OF SALTED WATER to the boil. Add the spaghetti and stir. Cook according to the packet instructions, until the pasta is al dente. About 30 seconds before the end of the cooking time, add the peas to warm through.

MEANWHILE, BEAT THE EGGS with the cream in a bowl. Sauté the pancetta in a pan with the olive oil.

DRAIN THE PASTA AND PEAS and put them back in the pan. Add the pancetta, then pour in the eggs and cream and put the pan over the heat for 30 seconds–1 minute. Season and finish with the parsley and Parmesan. Serve immediately.

SPAGHETTI WITH PUTTANESCA SAUCE

The spicier this is the better, so add as much chilli and garlic as you like.

2 tbsp olive oil
2 garlic cloves, crushed
1 x 400g can of tomatoes
5 salted anchovies
2 pinches of dried chillies
20 baby capers
375g dried spaghetti
10 black olives, chopped
2 tbsp chopped flatleaf
  parsley
50g Parmesan cheese,
  freshly grated

SERVES 4

HEAT THE OLIVE OIL in a pan, add the garlic and sauté until soft but not brown. Add the tomatoes, anchovies, chillies and capers and simmer until you have a thick sauce.

BRING A LARGE PAN OF SALTED WATER to the boil. Add the spaghetti and stir. Cook according to the packet instructions, until the pasta is al dente.

DRAIN THE PASTA, put it back in the pan and toss with the tomato sauce, chopped black olives and flatleaf parsley. Finish with freshly grated Parmesan and serve immediately.

SPAGHETTI WITH SARDINES

I love seafood with pasta , but don't add cheese – it doesn't need it.

350g dried spaghetti
2 tbsp olive oil
1 garlic clove, finely sliced
pinch of dried chilli
250g cherry tomatoes,
    cut in half
12 fresh sardines,
    scaled and filleted
grated zest of 1 lemon
1 tbsp chopped parsley
1 tbsp chopped basil
salt and freshly ground
    black pepper

SERVES 4

BRING A LARGE PAN OF SALTED WATER to the boil. Add the spaghetti and stir. Cook according to the packet instructions, until the pasta is al dente.

MEANWHILE, HEAT A TABLESPOON OF OLIVE OIL in a sauté pan and add the garlic and dried chilli. Add the cherry tomatoes and cook for 5 minutes so they start to break down and form a sauce. Season with salt and pepper. To finish, add the sardines on top and cook for a couple of minutes over a low heat.

DRAIN THE PASTA, put it back in the pan and toss it with the sardine and tomato sauce. Finish with the rest of the olive oil, the lemon zest and the chopped herbs and serve immediately.

LINGUINE WITH RADICCHIO AND CHORIZO

You can get fantastic chorizo in Britain now and it's great with pasta.

375g dried linguine
1 tbsp olive oil
100g chorizo, cut into discs
2 tsp capers
½ tsp chopped chilli
1 garlic clove, crushed
½ radicchio, shredded
handful of fresh basil, torn
freshly grated Parmesan
    cheese, for serving
salt and freshly ground
    black pepper

SERVES 4

BRING A LARGE PAN OF SALTED WATER to the boil. Add the linguine and stir. Cook according to the packet instructions, until the pasta is al dente.

HEAT THE OLIVE OIL in a pan and sauté the chorizo, then add the capers, chilli and garlic. Stir in the shredded radicchio and torn basil, then season.

DRAIN THE PASTA and put it back in the pan. Toss with the chorizo sauce and serve immediately with the Parmesan.

LINGUINE WITH RED MULLET CAPERS AND LEMON

Use a non-stick pan for cooking the fish so it doesn't stick when you come to toss everything together.

375g linguine
1 tbsp olive oil
½ red chilli, seeded and
    chopped
1 garlic clove, chopped finely
4 x 70g red mullet fillets,
    each cut into 5 thin strips
25g capers
150ml white wine
grated zest of 1 lemon
juice of ½ lemon
small handful of basil
1 tbsp chopped flatleaf
    parsley
salt and freshly ground
    black pepper

SERVES 4

BRING A LARGE PAN OF SALTED WATER to the boil. Add the linguine and stir. Cook according to the packet instructions, until the pasta is al dente.

HEAT THE OIL IN A FRYING PAN and sauté the chilli and garlic. Don't let them brown.

ADD THE RED MULLET to the pan and sauté briefly until cooked, then add the capers and white wine. Season with salt and pepper.

DRAIN THE LINGUINE and add it to the mullet. Add the lemon zest and juice and the herbs and toss gently. Serve immediately.

FIG TAGLIATELLE

350g dried tagliatelle
100ml olive oil
8 fresh figs, skin on, sliced
150ml double cream
handful of fresh basil,
    chopped
grated zest of 2 lemons
salt and freshly ground
    black pepper

SERVES 4

BRING A LARGE PAN OF SALTED WATER to the boil. Add the tagliatelle and stir. Cook according to the packet instructions, until the pasta is al dente.

MEANWHILE HEAT THE OLIVE OIL in another pan, add the figs and heat them through very gently.

DRAIN THE PASTA and put it back in the pan. Add the double cream and heat it through gently with the pasta. Add the figs, fresh basil and the lemon zest, season and serve immediately.

FUSILLI WITH SPROUTING BROCCOLI, CHILLI AND GARLIC

The classic version of this dish uses orecchiette – the ear-shaped pasta from Puglia – but I've adapted it for serving with fusilli.

250g sprouting broccoli,
   broken into small florets
375g dried fusilli
4 tbsp olive oil
1 tsp finely chopped chilli
2 garlic cloves, finely sliced
handful of freshly grated
   Pecorino cheese (optional)
salt and freshly ground
   black pepper

SERVES 4

BRING A LARGE PAN OF SALTED WATER to the boil and cook the broccoli florets until tender. Remove the broccoli, keep the cooking water in the pan and bring it back to the boil.

ADD THE PASTA TO THE PAN and stir. Cook according to the packet instructions, until the pasta is al dente.

HEAT 2 TABLESPOONS OF THE OLIVE OIL in a frying pan and sauté the chilli and garlic, without colouring. Add the cooked broccoli, season and set aside.

DRAIN THE PASTA, put it back in the pan and toss with the broccoli sauce. Finish with the grated Pecorino, if using, and the rest of the olive oil, then serve immediately.

FUSILLI WITH CAULIFLOWER, PINE NUTS AND RAISINS

1 small cauliflower,
   divided into florets
375g dried fusilli
1 tbsp olive oil
100g pancetta, chopped
100g pine nuts
100g raisins
2 tbsp chopped flatleaf
   parsley
freshly grated Parmesan
   cheese, for serving
salt and freshly ground
   black pepper

SERVES 4

BRING A LARGE PAN OF SALTED WATER to the boil and cook the cauliflower florets until soft. Remove the cauliflower, keep the cooking water in the pan and bring it back to the boil.

ADD THE PASTA TO THE PAN and stir. Cook according to the packet instructions, until the pasta is al dente.

HEAT THE OLIVE OIL in a frying pan and sauté the pancetta. Add the pine nuts and raisins and cook while the pasta is boiling. Add the cauliflower and season.

DRAIN THE PASTA and put it back in the pan. Add the cauliflower and pancetta mixture and toss everything together. Finish with the flatleaf parsley and serve immediately with freshly grated Parmesan.

PASTA WITH WALNUT SAUCE

200g shelled walnuts
2 tbsp breadcrumbs
25g butter
100ml double cream
375g linguine or tagliatelle
50g Parmesan cheese,
   freshly grated
1 tbsp chopped flatleaf
   parsley
salt and freshly ground
   black pepper

SERVES 4

WET THE WALNUTS in boiling water to soften them slightly. Place them in a pestle and mortar and pound them to a purée. Add the breadcrumbs and butter.

TIP THE WALNUT MIXTURE into a bowl and add the cream. If it still seems dry, add a touch more cream. Season with salt and pepper.

BRING A LARGE PAN OF SALTED WATER to the boil. Add the pasta and stir. Cook according to the packet instructions, until the pasta is al dente.

DRAIN THE PASTA, put it back in the pan and toss with the walnut sauce. Finish with freshly grated Parmesan and chopped parsley, then serve immediately.

TAGLIATELLE WITH SALAMI, HAZELNUTS AND TREVISO

Red chicory, from Treviso in northern Italy, is only available
in autumn, but you can use radicchio instead for this dish.

25g hazelnuts
1 tbsp olive oil
1 banana shallot, finely
    chopped
100g salami, diced
250g cherry tomatoes
375g tagliatelle
1 treviso, sliced
1 tbsp chopped flatleaf
    parsley
freshly grated Parmesan
    cheese, for serving
salt and freshly ground
    black pepper

SERVES 4

TOAST THE HAZELNUTS gently in a pan on top of the stove or
in the oven. Tip them into a clean cloth and rub off the skins.
Chop the hazelnuts and set aside.

HEAT THE OLIVE OIL in a frying pan and lightly sauté the shallot.

ADD THE SALAMI and sauté for 1 minute to release the oil. Add
the cherry tomatoes and sauté until they start to blister, then
continue to cook for 5 minutes to make a thick sauce. Season
with salt and pepper.

BRING A LARGE PAN OF SALTED WATER to the boil. Add the
tagliatelle and stir. Cook according to the packet instructions,
until the pasta is al dente.

DRAIN THE TAGLIATELLE, toss with the sauce and add the chopped
hazelnuts, treviso and parsley. Serve with freshly grated Parmesan.

MACARONI CHEESE

If you don't have any Cheddar, use up any odds and ends
of cheese you have in the fridge – even blue cheese.

400g dried macaroni
25g butter, plus 1 tbsp
   for cooking the leeks
25g flour
500ml milk
200g Montgomery Cheddar,
   freshly grated
2 leeks, washed, halved
   and sliced
100g pancetta, chopped
1 tbsp chopped flatleaf
   parsley
100g Parmesan cheese,
   freshly grated
salt and freshly ground
   black pepper

SERVES 4

BRING A LARGE PAN OF SALTED WATER to the boil. Add the
macaroni and stir. Cook according to the instructions on
the packet, until the pasta is al dente. Preheat the oven to
200°C/Fan 180°C/Gas mark 6.

MELT THE 25G OF BUTTER in another pan, then stir in the flour
and cook for 1 minute. Add the milk gradually, whisking it in until
you have a smooth white sauce. Season with salt and pepper, then
add the cheddar cheese and whisk again.

TO COOK THE LEEKS, melt the remaining butter in a pan and
add the sliced leeks and pancetta. Sauté until the leeks are soft
and the pancetta is cooked.

DRAIN THE PASTA and put it back in the pan, then mix in the
cheese sauce, leeks, pancetta and parsley. Pour everything into an
ovenproof dish and top with the grated Parmesan. Bake in the hot
oven for 15 minutes until golden brown and starting to bubble.

MACARONI WITH ASPARAGUS, CREAM AND HAM

You can't beat English asparagus, so only make this when it is in season.

500g fresh asparagus
375g macaroni or
    small penne
50g butter
200g cooked ham,
    sliced into strips
225ml double cream
50g Parmesan cheese,
    freshly grated
salt and freshly ground
    black pepper

SERVES 4

FIRST PREPARE THE ASPARAGUS. Break off the tough ends and then cut the stalks in two. Bring a pan of salted water to the boil, add the asparagus and cook until just tender. Drain, refresh in cold water and set aside.

BRING A LARGE PAN OF SALTED WATER to the boil. Add the macaroni and stir. Cook according to the packet instructions, until the pasta is al dente.

MELT THE BUTTER in a separate pan, add the cooked asparagus and gently toss it in the butter. Add the ham and allow it to heat through. Pour in the cream and bring to the boil, then turn down the heat.

DRAIN THE PASTA and put it back in the pan. Gently mix in the asparagus, cream and ham sauce, season to taste and add freshly grated Parmesan.

PENNE WITH GREEN OLIVES, ANCHOVIES AND ROCKET

This is a very easy pasta dish and you'll have most of the ingredients to hand in your store cupboard.

375g dried penne
1 tbsp olive oil
250g cherry tomatoes
1 bag of rocket leaves
8 salted anchovies, chopped
50g pitted green olives, chopped
1 tbsp chopped basil
freshly grated Parmesan cheese, for serving
salt and freshly ground black pepper

SERVES 4

BRING A LARGE PAN OF SALTED WATER to the boil. Add the penne and stir. Cook according to the packet instructions, until the pasta is al dente.

HEAT THE OLIVE OIL in a pan, add the tomatoes and cook them gently while the pasta is boiling.

DRAIN THE PASTA and put it back in the pan. Add the rocket, anchovies, olives and basil to the tomatoes and season. Toss with the pasta and serve with freshly grated Parmesan.

PENNE WITH PEAS, ANCHOVIES AND TICKLEMORE

You can use ricotta salata, a sheep's milk cheese from Sardinia, instead of Ticklemore if you like. And without the anchovies, this is a great dish for vegetarians.

100g fresh or frozen peas
100g fresh or frozen
  broad beans
375g dried penne
3 tbsp olive oil
2 small courgettes, sliced
50g Ticklemore cheese,
  sliced
1 tbsp chopped mint
8–12 white marinated
  anchovies
salt and freshly ground
  black pepper

SERVES 4

BRING A PAN OF SALTED WATER to the boil and cook the peas and beans until tender. Drain and set aside.

COOK THE PENNE in a large pan of boiling water according to the instructions on the packet, until the pasta is al dente. Heat 1 tablespoon of olive oil in a pan and sauté the courgettes.

DRAIN THE PASTA and put it back in the pan, then add the peas, broad beans, courgettes and the rest of the olive oil. To finish, add the Ticklemore cheese, chopped mint and season well. Serve immediately, adding some anchovies on top of each portion.

RIGATONI WITH FENNEL AND SAUSAGE

I love the spiciness of the sausage with the sweet tomatoes
in this dish. The sauce tastes even better the day after making,
so prepare it the day before if you can.

1 small fennel bulb
1 tbsp olive oil
1 small onion, sliced
250g Italian sausages (skins
    removed), cut into cubes
1 x 400g can of tomatoes
375g dried rigatoni
1 tbsp chopped flatleaf
    parsley
freshly grated Parmesan
    cheese, for serving
salt and freshly ground
    black pepper

SERVES 4

TRIM THE FENNEL, removing any tough outer leaves and the core,
then cut into thin slices.

HEAT THE OLIVE OIL in a pan, add the onion and fennel and sauté
until they start to soften. Add the cubed sausages and sauté for
3–4 minutes. Pour in the tomatoes and cook for 10 minutes until
you have a nice thick sauce and the sausages are cooked through.
Season with salt and pepper.

MEANWHILE, BRING A LARGE PAN of salted water to the boil. Add
the rigatoni and stir. Cook according to the packet instructions,
until the pasta is al dente.

DRAIN THE PASTA, put it back into the pan and toss with the
sausage sauce. Finish with the parsley and serve with freshly
grated Parmesan.

RIGATONI WITH AUBERGINE

This is a lovely summery pasta recipe, which you can spice up
with some cumin and crushed fennel seeds if you like.

1 aubergine
2 tbsp olive oil
2 garlic cloves, crushed
100ml red wine vinegar
6 plum tomatoes, diced
375g dried rigatoni
125g ricotta salata,
    freshly grated
handful of basil leaves, torn
salt and freshly ground
    black pepper

SERVES 4

SLICE THE AUBERGINE lengthways, then pile the slices on top of
each other and cut them into strips measuring about 5 x 2.5cm.
Place them in a colander, season with salt and pepper and leave
to drain for 30 minutes.

HEAT THE OLIVE OIL in a pan, add the crushed garlic and sauté
without allowing it to colour. Add the aubergine slices and
sauté until they are a nice golden colour – you might need to
do this in batches so you don't overcrowd the pan.

WHEN ALL THE AUBERGINE SLICES are sautéed, put them back
in the pan. Pour in the red wine vinegar, add the diced plum
tomatoes and cook for 10 minutes to make a light sauce. Check
the seasoning.

BRING A LARGE PAN OF SALTED WATER to the boil. Add the
rigatoni and stir. Cook according to the packet instructions,
until the pasta is al dente.

DRAIN THE PASTA, put it back in the pan and toss with the
aubergine sauce. Add the grated ricotta and basil leaves, then
serve immediately.

GOATS' CHEESE AND SPINACH LASAGNE WITH PINE NUTS

This is a wonderful vegetarian main course. To make things really easy, buy precooked lasagne which you can put straight into the dish.

75g butter
75g flour
500ml milk
500g spinach
500g rocket leaves
300g precooked lasagne
    sheets
200g goats' cheese,
    crumbled
1 tbsp pine nuts
100g Parmesan cheese,
    freshly grated
salt and freshly ground
    black pepper

SERVES 4

MELT THE BUTTER in a pan and heat until it starts to foam. Add the flour and cook for 1 minute, then gradually add the milk, whisking after each addition to make a nice thick sauce. Season with salt and pepper.

PREHEAT the oven to 180°C/Fan 160°C/Gas 4.

HEAT THE SPINACH in a large pan with 2 tablespoons of water for about 2 minutes until it wilts. Remove and set aside to cool, then squeeze out as much moisture as you can.

TAKE AN OVENPROOF DISH, measuring about 30 x 20cm, and spread a ladleful of white sauce over the bottom. Cover with some sheets of lasagne, then add some spinach and rocket, then a sprinkling of goats' cheese. Continue building up the layers, finishing with lasagne and pour the rest of the white sauce on top. Sprinkle with pine nuts and Parmesan.

BAKE IN THE PREHEATED OVEN for 30 minutes until the lasagne is golden and bubbling.

WHITE ONION RISOTTO

This is a good risotto to serve with fish or chicken
as it blends well with other flavours.

knob of butter
2 tbsp olive oil
2 white onions, thinly sliced
1 small onion, chopped
350g risotto rice
200ml white wine
about 850ml hot Vegetable
  stock (see page 283)
200g cold butter, diced
100g Parmesan cheese,
  freshly grated
salt and freshly ground
  black pepper

SERVES 4

FIRST MAKE A WHITE ONION PURÉE. Melt the butter in a pan
with a tablespoon of the oil. Add the white onions and a pinch
of salt, then cook until the onions are soft and broken down.
Don't allow them to brown. Tip the onions into a food processor
and blitz to a purée.

HEAT THE REMAINING OIL in a large pan over a medium heat.
Add the small chopped onion and cook, stirring, until soft and
translucent, about 2 minutes. Stir in the rice and cook for a further
2 minutes. Turn up the heat and add the wine – it should sizzle as
it hits the pan. Cook for about 2 minutes to evaporate the alcohol.

ONCE THE LIQUID HAS REDUCED, begin adding the hot stock
a ladleful at a time over a medium heat, allowing each addition
to be absorbed before adding the next, and stirring continuously.
The rice should always be moist but not swimming in liquid. The
process of adding and stirring should take about 18 minutes.
When the rice is done, stir in the white onion purée.

REMOVE FROM THE HEAT and stir in the diced butter. Finish
with the Parmesan, then season well and serve.

WHITE PEACH AND PROSECCO RISOTTO

This might sound strange, but it's a perfect summer dish
so give it a whirl. It must be made with the ripest of peaches.
Don't even try making this with unripe fruit.

6 ripe white peaches
2 tbsp olive oil
1 small onion, chopped
350g risotto rice
200ml Prosecco
about 850ml hot Vegetable
    stock (see page 283)
100g cold butter, diced
100g Parmesan cheese,
    freshly grated
salt and freshly ground
    black pepper

SERVES 4

BRING A PAN OF WATER to the boil, add the peaches and blanch
them for a moment or two. Remove the peaches, peel them, then
dice the flesh and set aside.

HEAT THE OIL in a large pan over a medium heat. Add the onion
and cook, stirring, until soft and translucent, about 2 minutes. Stir
in the rice and cook for a further 2 minutes. Turn up the heat and
add the Prosecco – it should sizzle as it hits the pan. Cook for about
2 minutes to evaporate the alcohol.

ONCE THE LIQUID HAS REDUCED, begin adding the hot stock
a ladleful at a time over a medium heat, allowing each addition
to be absorbed before adding the next, and stirring continuously.
The rice should always be moist but not swimming in liquid.
The process of adding and stirring should take about 18 minutes.

TOWARDS THE END OF THE COOKING TIME, add the diced peaches
and cook for a further minute.

REMOVE FROM THE HEAT and stir in the diced butter. Finish with
the Parmesan, season well and serve.

SEAFOOD RISOTTO

The seafood is usually folded into this risotto, but if you want a change,
sauté the fish and shellfish and serve it on top of the cooked rice.

2 tbsp olive oil
1 small onion, chopped
350g risotto rice
200ml white wine
about 850ml hot Fish stock
   (see page 283)
200g prawns, shelled
200g monkfish tail, chopped
100g squid, cleaned and
   sliced
200g cold butter, diced
2 tbsp chopped flatleaf
   parsley
salt and freshly ground
   black pepper

SERVES 4

HEAT THE OIL in a large pan over a medium heat. Add the onion
and cook, stirring, until soft and translucent, about 2 minutes.
Stir in the rice and cook for a further 2 minutes. Turn up the heat
and add the wine– it should sizzle as it hits the pan. Cook for
about 2 minutes to evaporate the alcohol.

ONCE THE LIQUID HAS REDUCED, begin adding the hot stock
a ladleful at a time over a medium heat, allowing each addition
to be absorbed before adding the next, and stirring continuously.
The rice should always be moist but not swimming in liquid.
The process of adding and stirring should take about 18 minutes.

THREE MINUTES before the risotto is due to be ready, fold in the
seafood and fish and let it cook – try not to let it get too mushy.

REMOVE FROM THE HEAT and stir in the diced butter and flatleaf
parsley. Serve immediately. Some people like to add Parmesan to
seafood risotto, but I prefer to leave it out – up to you.

CHESTNUT AND TRUFFLE RISOTTO

Colin Buchan put this on the lunch menu at the York and Albany and it's one of the best risottos I've ever tasted. If you don't have a truffle, finish the risotto with a drizzle of truffle oil instead.

2 tbsp olive oil
1 small onion, chopped
350g risotto rice
200ml white wine
about 850ml hot Vegetable
    stock (see page 283)
250g cooked chestnuts
    (vacuum-packed are fine)
200g cold butter, diced
50g Parmesan cheese,
    freshly grated
1 tbsp chopped flatleaf
    parsley
1 truffle, finely chopped,
    or 1 tbsp truffle oil
salt and freshly ground
    black pepper

SERVES 4

HEAT THE OIL in a large pan over a medium heat. Add the onion and cook, stirring, until soft and translucent, about 2 minutes. Stir in the rice and cook for a further 2 minutes. Turn up the heat and add the wine – it should sizzle as it hits the pan. Cook for about 2 minutes to evaporate the alcohol.

ONCE THE LIQUID HAS REDUCED, begin adding the hot stock a ladleful at a time over a medium heat, allowing each addition to be absorbed before adding the next, and stirring continuously. The rice should always be moist but not swimming in liquid. The process of adding and stirring should take about 18 minutes.

CRUMBLE 200G OF THE CHESTNUTS and add them to the risotto for the last 4 minutes of the cooking time. Finely slice the remaining 50g of chestnuts.

WHEN THE RISOTTO IS DONE, remove it from the heat and stir in the cold butter. Finish with the Parmesan and parsley, then season well and serve garnished with some sliced chestnuts. Finish with a sprinkling of truffle or a drizzle of truffle oil.

RISOTTO WITH SQUID INK

I first ate this risotto in southern Italy and now always order it whenever I see it on a menu. It tastes wonderful and looks so dramatic.

2 tbsp olive oil
1 small onion, chopped
1 garlic clove, finely chopped
350g risotto rice
200ml white wine
about 850ml hot Fish stock
    (see page 283)
2 sachets of cuttlefish ink
200g cold butter, diced
300g baby squid or
    chipirones, cut into rings
2 tbsp chopped flatleaf
    parsley
 salt and freshly ground
    black pepper

SERVES 4

HEAT THE OIL in a large pan over a medium heat. Add the onion and garlic and cook, stirring, until soft and translucent, about 2 minutes. Stir in the rice and cook for a further 2 minutes. Turn up the heat and add the wine – it should sizzle as it hits the pan. Cook for about 2 minutes to evaporate the alcohol.

ONCE THE LIQUID HAS REDUCED, begin adding the hot stock a ladleful at a time over a medium heat, allowing each addition to be absorbed before adding the next, and stirring continuously. The rice should always be moist but not swimming in liquid. The process of adding and stirring should take about 18 minutes.

TOWARDS THE END OF THE COOKING TIME, add the packets of squid ink.

REMOVE FROM THE HEAT and stir in the diced butter and the squid – the squid will cook in the heat of the rice. Finish with flatleaf parsley, check the seasoning and serve immediately.

NETTLE RISOTTO

Pick your own nettles for one of the cheapest risottos you can make. Do wear gloves, though! You'll have more purée than you need, but it freezes well.

500g nettles
2 tbsp olive oil
1 small onion, chopped
350g risotto rice
200ml white wine
about 850ml hot Vegetable
    stock (see page 283)
200g cold butter, diced
100g Parmesan cheese,
    freshly grated
salt and freshly ground
    black pepper

SERVES 4

BRING A PAN OF WATER TO THE BOIL and blanch the nettles. Drain them, reserving some of the cooking liquid, and purée in a food processor. Add a little of the liquid if the purée seems too dry.

HEAT THE OIL in a large pan over a medium heat. Add the onion and cook, stirring, until soft and translucent, about 2 minutes. Stir in the rice and cook for a further 2 minutes. Turn up the heat and add the wine – it should sizzle as it hits the pan. Cook for about 2 minutes to evaporate the alcohol.

ONCE THE LIQUID HAS REDUCED, begin adding the hot stock a ladleful at a time over a medium heat, allowing each addition to be absorbed before adding the next, and stirring continuously. The rice should always be moist but not swimming in liquid. The process of adding and stirring should take about 18 minutes.

TOWARDS THE END OF THE COOKING TIME, add 6 tablespoons of nettle purée. Taste and add more if necessary.

REMOVE FROM THE HEAT and stir in the cold butter. Finish with the Parmesan, then season well and serve.

LEMON RISOTTO WITH BROWN SHRIMP

Brown shrimps are good and very easy to come by in this country. They freeze well, so keep a bag in your freezer ready to use when you want.

2 tbsp olive oil
1 small onion, chopped
350g risotto rice
200ml white wine
about 850ml hot Vegetable
    stock (see page 283)
200g cold butter, diced
grated zest of 2 lemons
salt and freshly ground
    black pepper

For the shrimp garnish
2 tbsp olive oil
1 garlic clove, chopped
½ red chilli, finely chopped
250g brown shrimp, peeled
75ml white wine
handful of chopped basil

SERVES 4

HEAT THE OIL in a large pan over a medium heat. Add the onion and cook, stirring, until soft and translucent, about 2 minutes. Stir in the rice and cook for a further 2 minutes. Turn up the heat and add the wine– it should sizzle as it hits the pan. Cook for about 2 minutes to evaporate the alcohol.

ONCE THE LIQUID HAS REDUCED, begin adding the hot stock a ladleful at a time over a medium heat, allowing each addition to be absorbed before adding the next, and stirring continuously. The rice should always be moist but not swimming in liquid. The process of adding and stirring should take about 18 minutes.

TO PREPARE THE GARNISH, heat the olive oil in a separate pan and sauté the garlic and chilli. Add the shrimp and cook for a couple of minutes, then pour in the white wine and let it sizzle for a minute or two over a high heat. Finish with the basil and season well.

WHEN THE RISOTTO IS READY, remove it from the heat and stir in the cold butter and lemon zest. Serve with a helping of the shrimp garnish on each portion.

PEA AND PANCETTA RISOTTO

I first used this pancetta garnish to enliven a pasta dish and then found it worked equally well as a finishing touch on risotto.

2 tbsp olive oil
1 small onion, chopped
350g risotto rice
200ml white wine
about 850ml hot Vegetable
  stock (see page 283)
400g frozen peas
200g cold butter, diced
100g Parmesan cheese,
  freshly grated
salt and freshly ground
  black pepper

For the garnish
2 tbsp oil
200g pancetta, chopped
1 onion, finely chopped

SERVES 4

HEAT THE OIL in a large pan over a medium heat. Add the onion and cook, stirring, until soft and translucent, about 2 minutes. Stir in the rice and cook for a further 2 minutes. Turn up the heat and add the wine– it should sizzle as it hits the pan. Cook for about 2 minutes to evaporate the alcohol.

ONCE THE LIQUID HAS REDUCED, begin adding the hot stock a ladleful at a time over a medium heat, allowing each addition to be absorbed before adding the next, and stirring continuously. The rice should always be moist but not swimming in liquid. The process of adding and stirring should take about 18 minutes. Add the peas towards the end of the cooking time so that they warm through.

MEANWHILE, MAKE THE GARNISH. Heat the olive oil in a separate pan and sauté the pancetta. Remove the pancetta from the pan, add the onion and cook until light golden brown.

WHEN THE RISOTTO IS READY, remove it from the heat and stir in the diced butter. Finish with the Parmesan, then season well and serve topped with the onion and pancetta mixture.

SPINACH AND GORGONZOLA RISOTTO

Gorgonzola is best for this risotto, but you can use any blue cheese.

2 tbsp olive oil
1 small onion, chopped
350g risotto rice
200ml white wine
about 850ml hot Vegetable
    stock (see page 283)
250g washed baby spinach,
    chopped
100g Gorgonzola, cubed
200g cold butter, diced
50g Parmesan cheese,
    freshly grated
salt and freshly ground
    black pepper

SERVES 4

HEAT THE OIL in a large pan over a medium heat. Add the onion and cook, stirring, until soft and translucent, about 2 minutes. Stir in the rice and cook for a further 2 minutes. Turn up the heat and add the wine – it should sizzle as it hits the pan. Cook for about 2 minutes to evaporate the alcohol.

ONCE THE LIQUID HAS REDUCED, begin adding the hot stock a ladleful at a time over a medium heat, allowing each addition to be absorbed before adding the next, and stirring continuously. The rice should always be moist but not swimming in liquid. The process of adding and stirring should take about 18 minutes.

FOUR MINUTES BEFORE the end of the cooking time, add the spinach and Gorgonzola.

WHEN THE RISOTTO IS DONE, remove it from the heat and stir in the cold butter. Finish with the Parmesan, then season well and serve.

RED WINE AND CHORIZO RISOTTO

I like the idea of using red wine in risotto as an alternative to the classic white and it always surprises people. Use good-quality chorizo, available in most supermarkets now.

2 tbsp olive oil
1 small onion, chopped
350g risotto rice
200ml red wine
about 850ml hot Chicken
    stock (see page 282)
200g chorizo, sliced
200g cold butter, diced
50g Parmesan cheese,
    freshly grated
1 tbsp chopped flatleaf
    parsley
salt and freshly ground
    black pepper

SERVES 4

HEAT THE OIL in a large pan over a medium heat. Add the onion and cook, stirring, until soft and translucent, about 2 minutes. Stir in the rice and cook for a further 2 minutes. Turn up the heat and add the wine – it should sizzle as it hits the pan. Cook for about 2 minutes to evaporate the alcohol.

ONCE THE LIQUID HAS REDUCED, begin adding the hot stock a ladleful at a time over a medium heat, allowing each addition to be absorbed before adding the next, and stirring continuously. The rice should always be moist but not swimming in liquid. The process of adding and stirring should take about 18 minutes.

MEANWHILE, fry the chorizo in a pan over medium heat, until the red juices run.

WHEN THE RISOTTO IS DONE, remove it from the heat and stir in the chorizo with all its juices and the cold butter. Finish with the Parmesan and parsley, then season well and serve.

VEGETARIAN
AND
SIDE DISHES

BRAISED FENNEL

This fennel dish (see picture opposite) is perfect
with fish and also goes well with chicken.

2 fennel bulbs
2 tbsp olive oil
200ml Vegetable or Chicken
  stock (see pages 282–283)
1 rosemary sprig
1 star anise
squeeze of lemon juice,
  for serving
salt and freshly ground
  black pepper

SERVES 4

CUT THE FENNEL into quarters or eighths, depending on size,
and season with olive oil and salt.

HEAT A RIDGED CAST-IRON GRILL PAN and brown the fennel
on both sides. Preheat the oven to 180°C/Fan 160°C/Gas mark 4.

TRANSFER THE FENNEL TO AN OVENPROOF DISH. Pour in the
stock and add the rosemary, star anise and seasoning. Bake for
about 25 minutes or until soft and tender. If necessary, top up
with more stock or water so the fennel doesn't dry out. Squeeze
over some lemon juice before serving.

BRAISED TREVISO

Treviso can have a slightly bitter flavour, hence the icing sugar,
but it's delicious when prepared properly. This goes well with duck.

6 heads of treviso
  or red chicory
1 tbsp icing sugar
50g butter
2 tbsp balsamic vinegar
salt and freshly ground
  black pepper

SERVES 4

SLICE THE TREVISO. Sprinkle the icing sugar on a plate and
press the slices into it until coated.

HEAT THE BUTTER in a large frying pan until it starts to bubble,
then add the slices of treviso and colour on each side for a couple
of minutes. If the butter and sugar start to caramelise and burn,
add a touch of water to cool the pan down.

ADD A LITTLE WATER and stir until it evaporates, then add the
balsamic vinegar and stir, scraping up all the sticky bits from
the bottom of the pan. Season and serve the treviso immediately
with the pan juices.

SPROUTING BROCCOLI WITH SHALLOTS AND MUSTARD

This is a fantastic way of cooking sprouting broccoli (see picture opposite). It's best served warm.

450g sprouting broccoli
2 garlic cloves, sliced
1 tbsp olive oil
3 banana shallots,
    sliced into thin discs
2 tbsp coarse grain mustard
3–4 tbsp Classic vinaigrette
    (see page 282)
salt and freshly ground
    black pepper

SERVES 4

TRIM THE TOUGH ENDS OF THE BROCCOLI stalks. Bring a pan of salted water to the boil, add the broccoli and cook until tender. Drain immediately and set aside at room temperature.

SAUTÉ THE GARLIC in olive oil, but do not allow it to brown.

TOSS THE BROCCOLI with the garlic and shallots, then add the mustard, vinaigrette and parsley. Season and serve.

CAULIFLOWER WITH TOMATOES AND OLIVES

A lovely light fresh vegetable dish, this can be spiced up with more mustard or cumin, or you can add turmeric if you like.

1 cauliflower
100ml Classic vinaigrette
    (see page 282)
½ tsp ground cumin
2 tsp Dijon mustard
15 black Niçoise olives
6 tomatoes, chopped
1 tbsp chopped flatleaf
    parsley
salt and freshly ground
    black pepper

SERVES 4

REMOVE THE LEAVES AND ROOTS from the cauliflower and divide into large florets. Bring a large pan of salted water to the boil, add the cauliflower florets and cook until tender.

MIX THE VINAIGRETTE with the cumin and mustard. Drain the cauliflower and dress it with the vinaigrette and mustard mixture while still warm so it absorbs the flavour.

TO FINISH, add the olives, tomatoes and parsley. Season to taste.

BRAISED CHICORY WITH PANCETTA AND PARMESAN

For extra crunch, add some breadcrumbs with the Parmesan. This dish is good with beef or venison or can be served by itself (see picture opposite).

2 tbsp olive oil
4 large heads of chicory
   (Belgian endive),
   cut in half lengthways
100g pancetta, chopped
125ml double cream
50g Parmesan cheese,
   freshly grated
salt and freshly ground
   black pepper

SERVES 4

HEAT THE OLIVE OIL in a frying pan, add the chicory and colour on both sides. Place in an ovenproof dish. Preheat the oven to 180°C/Fan 160°C/Gas mark 4.

ADD THE PANCETTA to the frying pan and sauté briefly, then add the cream and cook until slightly thickened and reduced. Season, then pour the pancetta and cream mixture over the chicory.

SPRINKLE WITH GRATED PARMESAN and bake in the preheated oven for 15–20 minutes or until the chicory is cooked and the topping is golden brown.

MINTED COURGETTES

Serve with chicken or by itself as a buffet dish. Best at room temperature, this tastes even better the day after it's made.

4 large courgettes
olive oil
3 tbsp Classic vinaigrette
   (see page 282)
1 tbsp chopped mint
shavings of Pecorino cheese
salt and freshly ground
   black pepper

SERVES 4

CUT THE COURGETTES into diagonal slices, about 1cm thick. Brush them with olive oil and season with salt and pepper.

HEAT A RIDGED CAST-IRON GRILL PAN and grill the courgette slices, a few at a time, on both sides. Put them in a bowl and cover with cling film so they continue to cook as they cool.

WHEN READY TO SERVE, toss the courgettes with the vinaigrette and garnish with chopped mint and shavings of Pecorino.

POTATO SALAD WITH WARM TALEGGIO

Baked Vacherin cheese can be used instead of Taleggio if you like. Just add it on top of the grilled potatoes (see picture opposite).

250g new potatoes
1 garlic clove, crushed
a few rosemary sprigs
2 tbsp olive oil
125g Taleggio cheese,
    thinly sliced
salt and freshly ground
    black pepper

SERVES 4

PUT THE POTATOES in a pan of cold salted water, bring to the boil and simmer until tender. Drain, allow to cool slightly, then cut them in half lengthways.

TOSS THE POTATOES with the crushed garlic, rosemary and olive oil, then season. Heat a griddle pan and cook the potatoes until they are nicely marked on both sides. Put them in a ovenproof dish, season and cover with the thin slices of Taleggio. Place under a hot grill until the cheese is bubbling.

PEAS WITH SAGE AND BABY GEM

People don't always think about cooking lettuce, but baby gem cook very successfully. This is great with the Olive-stuffed lamb on page 172.

300g frozen peas
2 baby gem lettuces
1 tbsp olive oil
1 banana shallot,
    finely chopped
2 sage leaves
1 tsp chopped marjoram,
    fresh if possible
salt and freshly ground
    black pepper

SERVES 4

BRING A PAN OF SALTED WATER to the boil and blanch the peas. Drain and set them aside.

CUT THE ROOTS OFF THE LETTUCES and divide them into leaves, removing any damaged outer leaves.

HEAT THE OLIVE OIL IN A PAN and sauté the shallot until soft. Add the lettuce and sauté briefly, then add the peas, sage and marjoram. Season and serve immediately.

POLENTA WITH POACHED EGG AND MUSHROOMS

This is a lovely comforting dish. You could add pesto or fresh herbs to the polenta if you like, or leave out the mushrooooms and just serve the eggs on the polenta.

100g instant polenta
1 tbsp olive oil
100g button mushrooms, sliced
1 tbsp white wine vinegar
2 eggs
25g butter, for finishing polenta
25g Parmesan cheese, freshly grated, plus extra to shave over finished dish
salt and freshly ground black pepper

SERVES 2

COOK THE POLENTA according to the instructions on the packet, then set aside.

HEAT THE OIL IN A FRYING PAN and cook the mushrooms until they are tender.

BRING A PAN OF WATER to the boil and add the white wine vinegar. Crack the eggs into separate bowls. Turn the heat down so the water is simmering gently and then give it a stir so it swirls in the pan. Add the eggs and cook for 3 minutes at a low simmer.

STIR THE BUTTER AND GRATED PARMESAN into the polenta, then serve it into bowls. Place the poached eggs on top, then the mushrooms and some shavings of Parmesan. Season and serve immediately.

STUFFED TOMATOES

Make this in summer when tomatoes are at their best.
Great served with the Côte de boeuf on page 160.

2 beef tomatoes
1 tbsp olive oil
200g breadcrumbs
4 anchovies
1 tsp chopped capers
1 tbsp chopped parsley
1 tsp crushed garlic
25g butter, melted
salt and freshly ground
    black pepper

SERVES 2

PREHEAT THE OVEN to 190°C/Fan 170°C/Gas mark 5.

CUT THE TOPS OFF THE TOMATOES and scoop out the insides.
Set the flesh aside, but discard the seeds.

PLACE THE TOMATOES in an ovenproof dish. Season, drizzle
with olive oil and bake in the preheated oven for 5 minutes.
Leave the oven on.

MIX THE BREADCRUMBS, anchovies, capers, parsley and garlic
with the melted butter, add the reserved tomato flesh and season
with salt and pepper. Stuff the tomatoes with this mixture and
drizzle with a touch more olive oil.

PUT THE TOMATOES BACK IN THE OVEN for 5 more minutes
until the filling is hot.

COURGETTE AND RICOTTA SLICE

This is a lighter version of lasagne and is delicious
served cold as well as hot.

50ml olive oil
1 garlic clove, crushed
3 medium courgettes,
    sliced into discs
50g butter
6 sheets of filo pastry
150g ricotta
2 tbsp chopped mint
salt and freshly ground
    black pepper

SERVES 4

HEAT A TABLESPOON OF OLIVE OIL in a pan and add the crushed
garlic and courgettes. Sauté until soft, then remove from the heat
and leave to cool. Preheat the oven to 190°C/Fan 170°C/Gas mark 5.

MELT THE BUTTER and mix with the rest of the olive oil. Place
a sheet of filo pastry on a wooden board and brush with oil and
butter. Lay another sheet halfway across and brush, then repeat
until all the sheets are used up.

PLACE THE COURGETTES a third of the way up the filo pastry,
add the ricotta on top, then the chopped mint. Season with salt
and pepper.

ROLL THE FILO PASTRY round the filling like a large sausage, with
the join at the base. Cook in the preheated oven for 20 minutes
until golden brown.

SPICED AUBERGINE

This is my version of caponata. The classic dish includes capers and anchovies which you can add if you like, but I prefer to keep it simple.

2 large aubergines
100ml olive oil
2 red onions, finely chopped
4 plum tomatoes, seeded
    and diced
2 tbsp red wine vinegar
good pinch of cumin
handful of basil leaves, torn
handful of coriander leaves,
    picked from the stems
1 tbsp pine nuts, lightly
    toasted in a pan
sea salt and freshly ground
    black pepper

SERVES 4

CUT THE AUBERGINES INTO CHUNKS about 2cm thick and put them in a colander. Add about ½ teaspoon of salt and leave the aubergines to drain for half an hour.

HEAT 25ML OF THE OLIVE OIL in a pan and sauté the red onions until soft. Add the tomatoes and cook until you have a nice little tomato and onion stew. Season, then remove and set aside.

ADD HALF OF THE REMAINING OLIVE OIL to the pan and sauté half the aubergine chunks until tender. Remove and drain them on kitchen paper, then add the rest of the oil to the pan and sauté the remaining aubergine.

PUT THE TOMATO AND ONION back into the pan with all the aubergine and add the red wine vinegar, cumin, basil and coriander. Mix everything well and finish with the pine nuts. Check the seasoning and serve.

POTATOES BOULANGÈRE

We serve this all the time at the York and Albany.
If you like, you can cook it the day before, then next day
cut it into slices and warm through in the oven.

knob of butter
1 thyme sprig
2 garlic cloves, crushed
3 medium onions,
   thinly sliced
4 large potatoes, thinly
   sliced
300ml Chicken stock
   (see page 282)
salt and freshly ground
   black pepper

SERVES 4

PREHEAT THE OVEN to 190°C/Fan 170°C/Gas mark 5.

MELT A KNOB OF BUTTER in a pan over a gentle heat. Add the
thyme, garlic and sliced onions and sauté until the onions are
softened. Season.

GREASE A DEEP BAKING DISH with plenty of butter. Add a layer
of sliced potatoes, then some of the onion and thyme mix.
Continue layering until all the ingredients are used, finishing
with a layer of potato.

POUR IN THE HOT STOCK – there should be enough to seep
through the top layer of potatoes when you press them down.

BAKE IN THE PREHEATED OVEN for 40 minutes or until the
potatoes are soft and evenly browned on top. Serve right away.

DEEP-FRIED ARTICHOKES

This is a lovely light starter or snack – great to serve with drinks.

8 baby artichokes
vegetable oil, for deep-frying
squeeze of lemon juice

For the chilli salt
25g salt
25g dried chilli powder

SERVES 4

PEEL THE STALKS of the artichokes from the stems to the top of the leaves. Slice off the top 5mm of the leaves and remove the chokes with a spoon. By hand or on a mandolin, cut the artichokes into very thin slices, about 2mm thick.

MIX THE SALT and chilli powder together and set aside.

FILL A DEEP PAN with vegetable oil and heat to 180°C – test by dropping in a cube of bread; it should sizzle. Fry the artichoke slices, a few at a time, until crisp and golden. Drain well and season with the chilli salt and a squeeze of lemon.

PIES
AND
GRATINS

SHEPHERD'S PIE

You can prepare the pie filling ahead of time, cool it and keep in the fridge until you're ready. Then add the potato topping and cook at 180°C/Fan 160°/Gas 4 for 35 minutes.

500g boneless lamb
   shoulder or minced lamb
4 tbsp vegetable oil
2 large carrots, chopped
1 large onion, finely
   chopped
2 garlic cloves, chopped
1 leek, finely chopped
1 celery stick, finely chopped
2 tsp chopped thyme leaves
2 tbsp tomato purée
Worcestershire sauce
600ml Chicken stock
   (see page 282)
salt and freshly ground
   pepper

For the topping
600g Desiree potatoes
100ml milk
100g butter
2 egg yolks

SERVES 4

IF USING LAMB SHOULDER, trim any fat off the lamb and cut it into rough 2.5cm cubes. Season the cubes with salt and pepper.

HEAT HALF THE OIL in a heavy-based frying pan, and once it is smoking hot, brown the lamb shoulder or mince in batches, taking care not to overcrowd the pan or the meat will stew and not brown. Add more oil if needed. Once all the lamb is nicely coloured, remove it from the pan and set aside. Discard the oil.

ADD THE REST OF THE OIL to the hot pan. Add the carrots, onion, garlic, leek, celery and thyme and cook for 5 minutes. Add the tomato purée and cook for a further 2 minutes. Put the lamb back into the pan and add a splash of Worcestershire sauce, then the stock. Cook for another 30 minutes until the lamb is tender, the carrots cooked and the sauce has thickened. Season to taste.

PEEL AND DICE THE POTATOES and cook them in a pan of salted boiling water for 10–12 minutes. While they are cooking, gently heat the milk in a small pan. Once the potatoes are cooked, drain off all the water and then add the butter and hot milk to the pan. Take the pan off the heat, work the potatoes into a smooth purée and then add the egg yolks and mix them in well. Preheat the oven to 180°C/ Fan 160°C/Gas mark 4.

SPOON THE LAMB AND VEGETABLES into an ovenproof dish measuring roughly 23 x 23 x 5cm, or a round pie dish, and cover with the potato topping. Bake in the preheated oven for 20–25 minutes or until the top is golden and the meat is bubbling up at the sides.

FISH PIE

The sliced potato topping on this pie looks good
and makes a change from the usual mash.

300ml milk
5 white peppercorns
1 bay leaf
1 thyme sprig
700g white fish, such as
    pollock, hake or ling
150g salmon
75g butter
75g flour
2 tbsp chopped flatleaf
    parsley
150g peeled prawns
salt and freshly ground
    black pepper

For the topping
2 large potatoes
50g butter

SERVES 4

HEAT THE MILK in a pan with the peppercorns, bay leaf and
thyme. Remove from the heat, add the white fish and salmon
and leave to poach until just cooked.

WHEN THE FISH IS READY, lift it out with a slotted spoon and
set aside. Strain the herbs and peppercorns from the cooking
liquid and set the liquid aside. Preheat the oven to 180°C/Fan
160°C/Gas mark 4.

TO MAKE THE WHITE SAUCE, melt the butter in a separate pan,
add the flour and cook for 2 minutes. Slowly pour in the reserved
cooking milk and stir to make a smooth white sauce. Season with
salt and pepper.

GENTLY FLAKE THE FISH and place it in an ovenproof dish. Add
the chopped parsley and the prawns and pour in enough white
sauce to cover the fish.

PEEL THE POTATOES and cut them into very thin slices – about
2mm. Use a mandolin slicer if you have one. Carefully layer the
slices over the fish so they look like fish scales. Dot with butter
and season.

COOK THE PIE for 25 minutes in the preheated oven until golden
brown and starting to bubble. If you want to brown the top a little
more, turn the oven up for the last 5 minutes of cooking or put
the dish under a hot grill for a few minutes.

POTATO AND CELERIAC GRATIN

This is good with roast meat. Bring the dish to the table to serve family style.

knob of butter, for
    greasing the dish
100g pancetta
2 garlic cloves, chopped
2 medium onions, sliced
1 tsp chopped rosemary
1 tsp chopped thyme
4 medium potatoes,
    very finely sliced
1 celeriac, very finely sliced
200ml double cream
2 tbsp breadcrumbs
2 tbsp freshly grated
    Parmesan cheese
salt and freshly ground
    black pepper

SERVES 4

PREHEAT THE OVEN to 190°C/Fan 170°C/Gas mark 5. Generously butter an ovenproof dish.

SAUTÉ THE PANCETTA, GARLIC AND ONIONS in a pan until soft. Add the chopped herbs and mix well.

TIP THE PANCETTA MIXTURE into a big bowl, add the potato and celeriac slices and mix everything together well. Season with salt and pepper, pour over the double cream and press down lightly. Bake in the preheated oven for 25–30 minutes until the potatoes are soft.

PREHEAT THE GRILL. Mix the breadcrumbs and Parmesan and sprinkle them over the gratin. Put the dish under the grill until the top is golden brown.

BUBBLE AND SQUEAK

Perfect made with the leftovers from Christmas dinner or the Sunday roast.

50ml olive oil, plus 1 tbsp
2 spring onions, chopped
2 garlic cloves, chopped
leftover mashed potatoes
leftover cooked cabbage
1 tsp ground cumin
1 tbsp chopped parsley
flour
salt and freshly ground
    black pepper

SERVES 2-4

HEAT THE TABLESPOON OF OLIVE OIL in a pan and sauté the spring onions and garlic.

MIX THE LEFTOVER MASH AND CABBAGE in a bowl, then add the cumin, parsley and sautéed spring onions. Season with salt and pepper. Mould the mixture into cakes and roll in flour.

HEAT THE 50ML OF OLIVE OIL in a pan and fry the bubble and squeak cakes until golden brown.

ONION TART WITH ROCKET AND CHEDDAR

The key to success with this tart is to make sure you have plenty of onion filling. If there's too much egg and not enough onion you end up with an omelette instead of a tart. Make this in a tart tin or cut the pastry into an oblong and cook on a baking sheet.

250g shortcrust pastry
(see page 282)
1 tbsp olive oil
4 medium onions,
finely sliced
3 eggs
150ml double cream
2 tbsp chopped flatleaf
parsley
50g rocket leaves
100g Cheddar cheese,
freshly grated
salt and freshly ground
black pepper

SERVES 4

ROLL OUT THE PASTRY and use it to line a 20cm tart tin. Leave to chill in the fridge for 30 minutes.

PREHEAT THE OVEN to 190°C/Fan 170°C/Gas mark 5. Cover the pastry with a piece of baking parchment and fill it with baking beans, rice or dried pasta. Bake in the oven for 15 minutes, then remove the beans and paper and bake for another 5 minutes. Remove from the oven and leave to cool.

HEAT THE OLIVE OIL in a pan and sauté the onions until soft and lightly coloured. Leave to cool, then spread them over the pastry.

WHISK THE EGGS AND CREAM together, then add the parsley, rocket and grated Cheddar. Season with salt and pepper.

SPREAD THIS OVER THE ONIONS and cook the tart in a preheated oven at 190°C/Fan 170°C/Gas mark 5 for 20 minutes.

WILD MUSHROOM TART

Use any sort of mushrooms for this tart, which makes a delicious starter.

200g puff pastry
300g mixed wild
 mushrooms
2 tbsp olive oil
2 garlic cloves, crushed
1 tbsp chopped flatleaf
 parsley
2 tbsp freshly grated
 Parmesan cheese
salt and freshly ground
 black pepper

SERVES 4

ROLL OUT THE PUFF PASTRY into a rough circle about 25cm in diameter and prick the surface with a fork. Preheat the oven to 190°C/Fan 170°C/Gas mark 5.

PUT THE PASTRY on a baking sheet and bake in the preheated oven for about 15 minutes until golden brown. Remove and leave to cool.

CLEAN AND TRIM THE MUSHROOMS. Brush off any dirt and wipe them clean, or if they are very dirty, wash them in cold water, drain and dry. Cut the mushrooms into thick strips.

HEAT THE OLIVE OIL in a pan and sauté the mushrooms with the crushed garlic. Season and add the flatleaf parsley.

SPOON THE MUSHROOMS onto the puff pastry and sprinkle over the Parmesan. Cut into slices like a pizza and serve immediately.

BRAISED SWISS CHARD WITH FONTINA AND MUSHROOMS

This makes a lovely supper dish by itself and also makes a good accompaniment to roast meat, chicken or fish.

500g Swiss chard
juice of ½ lemon
1 tbsp olive oil
250g wild mushrooms
1 garlic clove, chopped
25g butter
25g flour
300ml milk, warmed
150g Fontina cheese,
   freshly grated
30g Parmesan cheese,
   freshly grated
30g breadcrumbs
salt and freshly ground
   black pepper

SERVES 4

REMOVE THE LEAVES FROM THE CHARD and trim the stalks. Bring a pan of salted water to the boil, add the lemon juice, then blanch the stalks until tender. Drain and set aside.

HEAT THE OLIVE OIL in a frying pan and sauté the mushrooms until golden. Add the garlic, then the chard stalks and finally the leaves and stir everything well. Preheat the oven to 180°C/ Fan 160°C/Gas mark 4.

MELT THE BUTTER IN A SMALL PAN, add the flour and cook for 2 minutes. Slowly add the milk and whisk to make a thick sauce. Season with salt and pepper, then add the Fontina and allow to melt.

MIX THE SAUCE WITH THE CHARD and mushrooms and pour into a buttered ovenproof dish. Sprinkle over the grated Parmesan and breadcrumbs.

BAKE IN THE PREHEATED OVEN for 20 minutes until heated through and golden brown on top.

MEAT
AND
POULTRY

CHICKEN WITH CHORIZO, PEPPERS AND SAGE

Ask your butcher to joint the chicken into legs, thighs and breasts for you and cut the breasts in half. This can be served hot or warm and it's also great cold the next day.

1 large corn-fed chicken,
    jointed as above
3 tbsp olive oil
3 red peppers
100g chorizo, peeled
    and sliced
2 garlic cloves, crushed
1–2 tbsp chopped sage
2 tsp chopped thyme
1 lemon
salt and freshly ground
    black pepper

SERVES 4

SEASON ALL THE PIECES OF CHICKEN with salt and pepper. Heat 2 tablespoons of the olive oil in a large non-stick frying pan and brown the chicken on both sides for 4–5 minutes. When all the chicken pieces are nice and golden, remove them from the pan and set aside.

CUT EACH PEPPER into 4 lengthways and discard the seeds and white flesh. Roughly dice the peppers into 2.5cm squares. Heat another tablespoon of olive oil in a frying pan and cook the chorizo for 2–3 minutes. Add the peppers, garlic, sage and thyme to the pan and cook for another 2 minutes. Preheat the oven to 180°C/ Fan 160°C/Gas mark 4.

POUR THE CHORIZO and pepper mixture into a roasting tin and place the chicken pieces on top. Zest the lemon and sprinkle over the chicken, then cut the lemon in half and squeeze over the juice of one half. Bake in the oven for 40–45 minutes, turning the chicken pieces halfway through the cooking time.

CHICKEN WITH GARLIC AND HERB BUTTER

This chicken recipe is so simple to do and you'll have lots of buttery, garlicky juices to serve with the meat.

1 whole garlic bulb, cut in half round the middle
1 lemon, cut in half
1 thyme sprig
1 rosemary sprig
1 free-range chicken, about 1.5kg
50g butter, plus extra for rubbing on the chicken
1 onion, roughly chopped
1 garlic clove, chopped
1 tbsp chopped shallot
½ tsp chopped rosemary and thyme
salt and freshly ground black pepper

SERVES 4

PREHEAT THE OVEN to 200°C/Fan 180°C/Gas mark 6.

PUT THE GARLIC, LEMON AND HERB SPRIGS in the cavity of the chicken, then rub butter all over the bird and season well. Sprinkle the onion over the base of a roasting tin and place the chicken on top.

ROAST in the preheated oven for 1 hour and 15 minutes, basting regularly. Remove the chicken from the oven and leave it to rest in a warm place for 5 minutes.

TO FINISH, put the 50g of butter in a small pan and heat until it bubbles. Add the chopped garlic, shallot and herbs, sauté for 1 minute, then pour this over the chicken before carving.

CHICKEN WITH OLIVES AND TOMATOES

I love the Mediterranean flavours in this chicken dish. Use capers instead of olives if you like or add a few anchovies. It's easy to serve too – just whack the dish on the table and let everyone help themselves.

4 corn-fed chicken legs,
   cut in half
1–2 tbsp olive oil
2 white onions, sliced
1 lemon, sliced
2 garlic cloves, crushed
4 thyme sprigs
50g butter
250g plum tomatoes,
   cut in quarters
50g black olives, pitted
   and cut in half
1 tbsp balsamic vinegar
salt and freshly ground
   black pepper

SERVES 4

HEAT THE OLIVE OIL in a large non-stick frying pan. Season the chicken pieces and lightly brown them in the pan. Do this in batches – if you overcrowd the pan the chicken will stew and not brown.

ONCE ALL THE CHICKEN IS LIGHTLY COLOURED, put it back into the pan and add the sliced onions, lemon, garlic and thyme. Add the butter and 100ml of water and continue to cook for about 10 minutes. Add the tomatoes and olives and cook for another 2–3 minutes until the chicken is just done. Mix everything together, then add the balsamic vinegar and cook for a further 1–2 minutes.

SPOON THE CHICKEN into a big bowl, then season with salt and pepper before serving.

POT-ROAST PHEASANTS

The game season in Britain gets better and better and most good butchers stock pheasants and other game birds. The season starts in August with grouse, then partridge and pheasants start appearing in autumn.

4 tbsp groundnut oil
2 pheasants, cleaned and
    ready to roast
100g pancetta, cut into
    large chunks
2 celery sticks, roughly
    chopped
2 carrots, roughly chopped
1 large onion, roughly
    chopped
1 head of garlic, cut in half
200ml white wine
1 thyme sprig
1 bay leaf
1 sage leaf
6 juniper berries, crushed
400ml Chicken stock
    (see page 282)
salt and freshly ground
    black pepper

SERVES 4

PREHEAT THE OVEN to 160°C/ Fan 140°C/Gas mark 3.

HEAT THE GROUNDNUT OIL in a large pan. Season the pheasants, add them to the pan and brown them on all sides.

REMOVE THE PHEASANTS and set aside. Add the pancetta, vegetables and garlic to the pan and brown them gently, then remove. Pour in the white wine and stir with a wooden spoon to scrape up all the sticky bits.

PUT THE PHEASANTS, vegetables and cooking juices into a large casserole dish. Add the herbs and juniper berries and pour in the chicken stock. Bring to the boil and cover with a lid or a circle of baking parchment. Cook in the preheated oven for about 1½ hours.

REMOVE FROM THE OVEN and leave the pheasants to rest for 10 minutes. Carve and serve with the warmed-through juices and the vegetables.

GUINEA FOWL WITH LEMON AND SAGE STUFFING

This stuffing is perfect with guinea fowl. If you have any left after stuffing the bird, you could shape it into small balls and add them to the roasting tin for the last 30 minutes of the cooking time.

1 guinea fowl
1 tbsp olive oil
squeeze of lemon juice
salt and freshly ground
    black pepper

Stuffing
1 tbsp olive oil
1 onion, chopped
100g pancetta, diced
25g butter
50g Japanese panko
    breadcrumbs
2 Cumberland sausages
50g flaked almonds
1–2 tbsp chopped sage
zest of 2 lemons

SERVES 4

FIRST MAKE THE STUFFING. Heat the olive oil in a frying pan and add the onion. Cook until soft and golden, then set aside. Add the diced pancetta to the pan and cook until the pancetta is crispy. In a separate pan, melt the butter until it is foaming, then add the breadcrumbs and cook until they are lightly toasted. Skin the sausages and put the meat in a bowl with the onions, pancetta, breadcrumbs and almonds. Add the chopped sage and lemon zest, then mix everything together well.

STUFF THE MIXTURE into the cavity of the guinea fowl and place in a roasting tin. Preheat the oven to 180°C/Fan 160°C/Gas mark 4.

RUB THE GUINEA FOWL all over with olive oil and season with salt and pepper. Cook the bird in the preheated oven for 1 hour and 10 minutes, or until it is cooked through and the stuffing is hot. Squeeze over some lemon juice and serve.

DUCK LEG STEW

If you're nervous of cooking duck, try this recipe
which uses only the legs and is very easy to do.

4 duck legs
4 Cumberland sausages
150g smoked streaky bacon,
    cut into strips
1 carrot, diced
1 onion, diced
2 garlic cloves, finely
    chopped
200ml Madeira wine
600ml Chicken stock
    (see page 282)
100g ditalini pasta
125g cherry tomatoes,
    halved
handful of flatleaf parsley,
    chopped
salt and freshly ground
    black pepper

SERVES 4

PREHEAT THE OVEN to 180°C/Fan 160°C/Gas mark 4. Trim
the excess fat from the duck legs, and season them with salt
and pepper.

PLACE THE DUCK LEGS, skin-side down, in a dry pan over a low
to medium heat. Cook for 10 minutes until the skin is brown and
the fat is running. Remove the duck legs, set them aside and tip
the excess fat into a bowl.

BROWN THE SAUSAGES in the pan, then remove them and leave
to cool slightly before cutting into thick slices. Set aside. Preheat
the oven to 180°C/Fan 160°C/Gas mark 4.

WARM A LITTLE OF THE DUCK FAT in a large pan or casserole that
can be put in the oven and cook the bacon until golden. Add the
diced carrot, onion and chopped garlic, mix everything together
well and cook for 6–8 minutes until soft. Pour in the Madeira and
stir to scrape up all the sticky bits from the bottom of the pan,
then cook until the liquid is reduced and sticky.

PUT THE DUCK LEGS and sausages back into the pan and pour in
the chicken stock. Bring the liquid to a simmer, then transfer the
pan to the preheated oven and cook for 35–40 minutes. The duck
legs should be tender and almost falling apart.

TAKE THE PAN OUT OF THE OVEN and carefully remove the legs
from the stock. Turn the oven up to 200°C/Fan 180°C/Gas mark 6.
Place the duck legs in a roasting tin, skin-side up, and put them
back into the oven to crisp up the skin – about 8 minutes.

BRING THE STOCK BACK TO THE BOIL, add the ditalini and simmer
for 9 minutes. Once the pasta is cooked, add the cherry tomato
halves and the chopped parsley.

SEASON THE STEW to taste and spoon it into bowls. Finally, add
a crispy duck leg on top and serve.

PORK WITH PRUNES

The idea for this came from my Swedish uncle who used to cook pork loin stuffed with prunes. I think the compote goes beautifully with the meat.

1.5kg pork loin, skin on
salt
olive oil, for rubbing
    on the meat

For the honey and
    mustard glaze
150ml honey
1 tbsp Dijon mustard
50ml white wine
50ml white wine vinegar

For the prune compote
1 tbsp olive oil
2 shallots, diced
1 Braeburn apple, peeled
    and chopped
zest and juice of 1 orange
20 prunes pitted, cut in half
1 tbsp chopped flatleaf
    parsley
1 tsp chopped lemon thyme

SERVES 4

PREHEAT THE OVEN to 180°C/Fan 160°C/Gas mark 4. Take a sharp knife and remove any excess fat from the pork loin. Score the skin, then rub it all over with salt and leave it to rest in the fridge for 1–2 hours.

BRUSH OFF THE EXCESS SALT and tie the pork loin in 4 or 5 places to hold it together. Use butchers' twine if you have it, but ordinary string is fine. Place the pork in a roasting tin, rub it with olive oil and then cook in the oven for 40–60 minutes.

PREPARE THE HONEY AND MUSTARD GLAZE while the pork is cooking. Heat the honey in a small saucepan and bring it to the boil. Add the mustard, white wine and vinegar and boil until the mixture has reduced to a slightly thick consistency.

REMOVE THE PORK FROM THE OVEN and baste it with the honey and mustard glaze. Return it to the oven and cook for another 30 minutes, basting with the glaze every 10 minutes.

TO MAKE THE PRUNE COMPOTE, heat the oil in a pan and fry the diced shallots until soft and golden. Add the chopped apple to the pan and cook for 3–4 minutes. Add the orange zest and the prunes to the pan and cook for another 2 minutes. Pour the orange juice into the pan and stir to scrape up all the crispy bits, then cook the mixture until it reaches a compote-like consistency. Finally, add the chopped parsley and lemon thyme.

ONCE THE PORK IS COOKED, leave it to rest for 10 minutes and serve with the prune compote.

ROAST PORK WITH SPINACH AND SPRING ONIONS

You can bring an Asian touch to this by sautéing the spring onions with a little chopped ginger and adding a touch of soy sauce to the spinach.

2kg pork loin
olive oil, for rubbing
    on the meat
1 bunch of spring
    onions, chopped
500g spinach
grated zest of 1 lemon
salt and freshly ground
    black pepper

SERVES 4

TAKE A SHARP KNIFE and remove any excess fat from the pork loin. Score the skin, then rub it all over with salt and leave it to rest in the fridge for 1–2 hours.

PREHEAT the oven to 220°C/Fan 200°C/Gas mark 7.

BRUSH ANY EXCESS SALT OFF THE PORK, place it in a roasting tin and rub with olive oil. Roast for 30 minutes, then turn the oven down to 190°C/Fan 170°C/Gas mark 5 and cook for another 50 minutes until the pork is done. Take the pork out of the oven and leave to rest for 15 minutes or so.

SAUTÉ THE SPRING ONIONS in a tablespoon of olive oil in a frying pan, then remove them and briefly sauté the spinach. Add a touch of olive oil and lemon zest to the vegetables, season and serve with the pork.

PORK BRAISED IN MILK

Ths might sound unusual but it is excellent, so give it a try.
The pan must be just big enough for the pork to fit. If the pan
is too large, the liquid will evaporate too much.

800g boneless pork shoulder
4 tbsp olive oil
30g butter
2 small onions, chopped
1 garlic clove, chopped
1 litre milk
1 thyme sprig
1 bay leaf
salt and freshly ground
    black pepper

SERVES 4

TRIM ANY EXCESS FAT and sinew off the pork with a sharp knife
and season with salt and pepper. Preheat the oven to 180°C/
Fan 160°C/Gas mark 4.

HEAT THE OLIVE OIL in a pan that has a lid and can be put into
the oven as well as used on the hob. Brown the pork on all sides,
then remove and set aside. Pour out the oil and discard it, then
add the butter to the pan and heat until it foams. Add the chopped
onions and garlic and cook for 3–4 minutes, then put the meat
back into the pan.

POUR IN THE MILK – it should just cover the meat – add the
thyme and bay leaf and bring to the boil. Cover the pan with
foil and the lid and cook in the preheated oven for 2–3 hours,
basting every hour.

ONCE THE MEAT IS SO TENDER that it is almost falling apart,
remove it from the milk and leave it to rest in a warm place,
covered with cling film.

PASS THE MILK through a fine conical sieve into a pan and bring
back to the boil. Cook until it starts to thicken and turn golden,
then check the seasoning. Do not let the sauce reduce too much
or it might split. If it does split, add a splash of cold milk and
whizz with a hand blender to bring the sauce back together.

CARVE THE PORK and serve it with the milk sauce.

SLOW-COOKED PORK BELLY

We have very good pork now in this country and it's worth buying
the best you can find − cheap pork is watery and doesn't taste good.

800g boneless pork belly,
    skin on
8 garlic cloves, unpeeled
5 shallots, cut in half
a few thyme sprigs
1 rosemary sprig
1 bay leaf
4 tbsp olive oil
salt and freshly ground
    black pepper

SERVES 4

PREHEAT THE OVEN to its maximum temperature. Dry the pork
with kitchen paper, making sure that the skin side is really dry.
Now take a sharp knife and score the skin side of the belly in both
directions. Rub the skin with salt, making sure to get some of it
into the slits.

CRUSH THE GARLIC CLOVES and mix them with the shallots,
herbs and olive oil in a bowl. Season with salt and pepper.

MAKE A NEST of three or four pieces of tin foil into which the pork
will fit in snugly. Put the nest on an oven tray, tip the vegetables
into the centre and then place the pork on top. Press the tin foil
into the sides of the pork, place it in the oven and immediately
turn the temperature down to 140°C/Fan 120°C/Gas mark 1.

COOK THE PORK for 3 hours, then reduce the oven temperature
to 120°C/Fan 100°C/Gas mark ½ and cook for another hour. If after
this time the crackling does not seem crispy enough, increase the
temperature to maximum again and cook until it is just crispy.

TAKE THE PORK OUT OF THE OVEN and leave it to rest for about
10 minutes before serving.

RABBIT WITH FENNEL, OLIVES AND ROSEMARY

This is a variation on the classic chicken cacciatore, made with rabbit. In fact, the original recipe probably used rabbit, which would have been less expensive than chicken.

2 tbsp olive oil
8 rabbit legs
1 onion, chopped
1 celery stick, chopped
2 garlic cloves, finely
    chopped
2 tbsp tomato purée
500ml Madeira
500ml Chicken stock
    (see page 282)
2 thyme sprigs
2 rosemary sprigs
2 bay leaves
1 tsp chopped rosemary
salt and freshly ground
    black pepper

For the fennel
2 fennel bulbs
2 tbsp olive oil
50g green olives, pitted
1 tsp chopped rosemary
2 tbsp honey
1 tbsp sherry vinegar
salt and freshly ground
    black pepper

SERVES 4

HEAT A TABLESPOON OF OLIVE OIL in a large frying pan and lightly colour the rabbit legs on all sides. Once the rabbit legs are golden, remove them from the pan and set them to one side. Discard the used oil and heat a tablespoon of fresh oil in the pan. Add the chopped vegetables and cook for 5 minutes, then add the tomato purée, season, and cook for a further 2 minutes.

ADD THE MADEIRA, chicken stock, herbs (except the chopped rosemary) and rabbit legs to the pan, then cover with a circle of greaseproof paper to keep in all the moisture. Simmer over a medium heat for 35–40 minutes.

PREPARE THE FENNEL. Preheat the oven to 180°C/Fan 160°C/Gas mark 4. Cut the fennel bulbs into quarters or sixths, depending on their size, and toss them in a bowl with olive oil, salt and pepper. Using a pan that can be put in the oven, fry the fennel until golden. Add the olives, rosemary and honey to the pan and mix well. Pour in the sherry vinegar and scrape up all the juices and sticky bits, then put the pan in the oven for 10–15 minutes, or until the fennel is just cooked.

ONCE THE RABBIT LEGS ARE DONE, remove them from the pan and set them to one side. Strain the braising juices through a sieve and discard the vegetables. Pour the juices back into the pan along with a dash of sherry vinegar, and reduce the sauce over a medium heat until it is thick and shiny. Put the rabbit legs back into the pan and coat them with the sauce. Tip the honey-glazed fennel into the pan with the rabbit, then serve.

VEAL STEAKS WITH LEMON AND CHIVES

If you stopped eating veal because of the rearing practices, try rose veal which is less intensively reared and so more humane. The meat is delicious too. Add a touch of sage if you like, as it goes well with the veal and lemon.

800g veal loin, sliced
    very thinly
2 tbsp plain flour
1 tbsp olive oil
30g butter
2 shallots, finely sliced
2 lemons
1–2 tbsp chives, roughly
    chopped
salt and freshly ground
    black pepper

SERVES 4

PLACE THE VEAL STEAKS between two sheets of cling film and pound them with a rolling pin or the bottom of a heavy frying pan until they are about 1cm thick.

SEASON THE STEAKS with salt and pepper and coat them with flour, shaking off any excess. Heat the olive oil in a pan and fry the veal steaks for about 2 minutes on each side. When they are coloured on both sides, take them out of the pan and leave them to one side.

MELT THE BUTTER in the pan until it starts to foam, then add the finely sliced shallots and the zest of both lemons. Cook for 2 minutes, then add the juice of 1 lemon and stir well. Finish with the chopped chives and season with salt and pepper. Pour the sauce over the veal steaks and serve with a squeeze of lemon.

VEAL CHEEKS

This is a great winter dish and can be made in a slow-cooker if you have one. Serve with some mash and greens to soak up the braising liquor.

8 small veal cheeks, trimmed and ready to cook
2 tbsp olive oil
4 shallots, sliced
½ head of garlic, chopped
4 thyme sprigs
12 black peppercorns
2 tbsp tomato purée
1 bottle of white wine
1 litre Chicken stock (see page 282))
splash of sherry vinegar
salt and freshly ground black pepper

SERVES 4

SEASON THE VEAL CHEEKS with salt and pepper. Heat a tablespoon of olive oil in a heavy-based frying pan and brown the cheeks on all sides. Remove the cheeks from the pan and set aside. Tip out the used oil.

ADD A TABLESPOON OF FRESH OIL to the pan. Add the sliced shallots, garlic, thyme and peppercorns and fry for 2–3 minutes. When the shallots are nice and golden, add the tomato purée and cook for another 2 minutes.

POUR IN THE WHITE WINE, stirring well to scrape up all the sticky bits, and cook for 15 minutes until the liquid is reduced and sticky.

PUT THE CHEEKS back into the pan, pour in the chicken stock and bring to the boil. Cover with a circle of greaseproof paper and leave to simmer over a low heat for 90 minutes.

IF YOU PREFER, you can cook the cheeks in the oven – preheat to 180°C/Fan 160°C/Gas mark 4. At the end of the cooking time the veal cheeks should be soft and almost falling apart.

REMOVE THE MEAT from the liquid and set aside. Pass the cooking liquid through a conical sieve, then pour it back into the pan and cook over a high heat until it has reduced and has a sauce-like consistency. This will take 10–15 minutes. Add a splash of sherry vinegar, then put the veal cheeks back into the sauce to warm through, then serve.

ROASTED VEAL WITH ONIONS AND LEMONS

700g rose veal shin
4 tbsp olive oil
3 medium onions,
    cut into quarters
2 lemons, cut into quarters
salt and freshly ground
    black pepper

SERVES 4–6

PREHEAT THE OVEN to 180°C/Fan 160°C/Gas mark 4.

REMOVE THE EXCESS FAT from the veal with a sharp knife, then season the meat with salt and pepper. Heat the olive oil in a large frying pan and colour the veal on all sides until golden.

PUT THE PAN INTO THE OVEN (or transfer the meat to a heated roasting tin) and add the onions and lemons. Cook the veal for 45–60 minutes, depending on the thickness of the meat. You can check if the meat is cooked by pricking the centre with a sharp knife. Take the knife out and feel it – it should be warm or hot to the touch. Once the veal is done, take it out of the oven and leave it to rest for 5 minutes in a warm place.

BRISKET WITH ONIONS AND TURNIPS

Brisket is an underused cut and well worth trying. When marinated and cooked carefully, it tastes fantastic.

1.2kg beef brisket, rolled and tied (ask your butcher to do this for you)
3 tbsp olive oil
1 litre Chicken stock (see page 282)
2 large onions, cut into wedges
2 large turnips, cut into wedges
10 garlic cloves, unpeeled
50ml balsamic vinegar
2 tbsp chopped flatleaf parsley
salt and freshly ground black pepper

For the marinade
½ bottle red wine
a few thyme sprigs
2 bay leaves
3 tbsp honey
½ head of garlic
1 carrot, chopped
1 onion, chopped

SERVES 4-6

MARINATE THE BRISKET for several hours, preferably overnight, before cooking. To do this, put the brisket and marinade ingredients in a bowl, cover with cling film and leave in the fridge. Turn the brisket several times to ensure it is evenly marinated.

TAKE THE MEAT OUT of the marinade, then separate the liquid from the vegetables and set both aside. Heat 2 tablespoons of olive oil in the casserole dish you're going to use to cook the meat and brown the brisket quickly on all sides. Remove the brisket and set it aside. Preheat the oven to 180°C/Fan 160°C/Gas mark 4.

TIP OUT THE USED OLIVE OIL and add a tablespoon of fresh oil to the pan. Add the vegetables from the marinade and brown them lightly for about 2 minutes. Put the brisket back into the pan, then add the marinade liquid and bring to the boil. Add the chicken stock and bring back to the boil. Cover the pot with a lid and braise in the preheated oven for 2–3 hours.

PUT THE ONIONS AND TURNIPS into a bowl along with the garlic cloves, salt, pepper and a drizzle of olive oil. About 30–35 minutes before the meat is due to be ready, tip the vegetables into a roasting tin and cook them in the same oven as the meat.

TEST THE BRISKET is ready by pricking it gently with a knife: if the meat does not offer any resistance, it is cooked through. Remove the meat and set it aside, then strain the cooking juices through a fine sieve, discarding the marinade vegetables. Put the juices and the vinegar into a pan and reduce over a medium heat for 8–10 minutes, or until you have a thick sauce. Check the seasoning.

ONCE THE ONIONS AND TURNIPS ARE COOKED, cover them with 2 tablespoons of the sauce so they are glazed and shiny, then add the chopped parsley. Carve the brisket and serve with the vegetables and another spoonful of the sauce.

SALT BEEF WITH DUMPLINGS

I love dumplings, which we often used to eat when I was a child, and they make a great alternative to potatoes.

1kg salt beef
1 large onion
1 bay leaf
12 black peppercorns
2 cloves
a few thyme sprigs
English mustard, to serve

Dumplings
110g self-raising flour (or
    100g plain flour plus
    1 tsp baking powder)
55g suet
2 tbsp chopped flatleaf
    parsley
2 tbsp fresh horseradish,
    grated
salt and freshly ground
    black pepper

SERVES 6

THE DAY BEFORE you want to cook the beef, put it into a large pan of cold water and leave to soak overnight to get rid of some of the salt. Next day, drain the beef, put it into a large saucepan and add enough water to cover it by 2.5–5cm.

CUT THE ONION into quarters and add it to the pan with the bay leaf, peppercorns, cloves and thyme sprigs. Bring the liquid to the boil and then turn it down to a simmer. If the liquid still tastes really salty after the first 10 minutes, drain it and start again. Simmer for 2½–3 hours, skimming any scum off the surface when necessary. Keep an eye on the water and top it up as needed.

REMOVE THE SALT BEEF from the pan, cover it with cling film and set it aside. Strain the poaching liquid through a sieve and pour it back into the pan – you will need it for cooking the dumplings.

TO MAKE THE DUMPLINGS, sieve the flour and add the remaining ingredients. Add cold water a little at a time until you have a slightly wet, sticky dough. Flour your hands and shape the mixture into 12 dumplings.

BRING THE POACHING LIQUID from the meat back to a simmer, drop in the dumplings, a few at a time, and cook them for 12 minutes. Drain well. Serve with the beef and a generous helping of English mustard.

CÔTE DE BOEUF

This dish always sells out when we put it on the menu at the
York and Albany. Just pile it onto a board and help yourselves.

2 x 450g beef rib steaks,
    bone in
4 tbsp olive oil
1 head of garlic, cut
    horizontally through
    the middle
a few thyme sprigs
50–100g butter

For the salad
2 shallots, finely chopped
20 cherry tomatoes,
    cut in half
small handful of chives,
    finely chopped
2 tbsp olive oil
1 tsp balsamic vinegar
salt and freshly ground
    black pepper

For the salsa verde
1 garlic clove
4 fresh anchovies in vinegar
2 tbsp capers
2 tbsp cornichons
4 tbsp olive oil
½ bunch of parsley, leaves
    only
1 tbsp red wine vinegar
salt and freshly ground
    black pepper

SERVES 4

TO MAKE THE SALSA VERDE, blend the garlic, anchovies, capers
and cornichons in a food processor. Add the olive oil and parsley
leaves, then blend again until a smooth paste forms. Add the red
wine vinegar and stir – the paste should have a smooth, runny
consistency, so add more oil if it's still too thick. Season with salt
and pepper to taste.

PREHEAT THE OVEN to 180°C/Fan 160°C/Gas mark 4. Coat the meat
on all sides with olive oil and season with salt and pepper. Grill the
steaks on a hot, ridged grill pan for 4 minutes on all sides, then
transfer them to a roasting tin. Add the garlic and put some thyme
and a cube of butter on top of each steak, then cook in the oven
for 8 minutes for medium-rare meat.

MAKE A SALAD with the shallots, cherry tomatoes and chives,
then dress with the olive oil, balsamic vinegar, salt and pepper.

ONCE THE BEEF IS COOKED, let it rest for a few minutes. Carve
each piece into 6 slices and serve with the salad and a big spoonful
of salsa verde. Quickly heat the cooking juices from the roasting
tin and pour over the meat to finish.

ROAST BEEF

Sirloin is cheaper than fillet but still an excellent tasty meat. It's off the bone, so very easy to carve, and any leftovers are great cold the next day.

800g beef sirloin
2 tbsp olive oil
1 large onion, sliced
1 thyme sprig, leaves
   picked from the stems
salt and freshly ground
   black pepper

SERVES 4

PREHEAT THE OVEN to 180°C/Fan 160°C/Gas mark 4. Using a sharp knife, trim any excess fat and sinew off the beef. Score the flap of fat with a knife and then tie the meat with butchers' twine or ordinary string in 4 or 5 places so it holds its shape. Season with salt and pepper.

HEAT THE OLIVE OIL in a pan and colour the beef on all sides until golden. Transfer the meat to a roasting tin and add the sliced onion and thyme. Finish cooking in the oven for 20–25 minutes for medium-rare meat. You can check if the meat is cooked by pricking the centre with a sharp knife. Take the knife out and feel it – it should be warm or hot to the touch. When the beef is cooked, cover it with foil and set it aside to rest.

ONCE THE BEEF HAS RESTED, carve and serve with braised treviso (see page 107).

BEEF AND ONION GRATIN

This one-pot wonder is a great supper dish. Just put everything in the pan and leave it to cook.

600g beef chuck meat
plain flour, for dusting
100ml vegetable oil
2 onions, sliced
2 garlic cloves, chopped
a few thyme sprigs
2 tbsp tomato paste
1 bottle of red wine
400ml Chicken stock
    (see page 282)
Worcestershire sauce
splash of balsamic vinegar
100g Japanese panko
    breadcrumbs or ordinary
    breadcrumbs
100g freshly grated
    Parmesan cheese
salt and freshly ground
    black pepper

SERVES 4

TRIM ANY EXCESS FAT and sinew from the meat with a sharp knife, then dice it into 2.5cm cubes. Season the meat with salt and pepper and toss it in plain flour.

POUR THE OIL into a pan and heat until smoking hot. Add the meat and brown it on all sides. Be sure not to overcrowd the pan – the meat must brown not stew. As the meat is browned, set it aside.

ADD THE ONIONS, garlic and thyme to the pan, then add the tomato paste and cook for 2 minutes. Pour in the red wine and stir, scraping up all the juices and sticky bits from the bottom of the pan. Continue until the liquid is reduced, then put the meat back in the pan and add the chicken stock.

COVER THE PAN WITH A LID and simmer for about 1½ hours. Finish with a splash of Worcestershire sauce and balsamic vinegar.

STRAIN THE LIQUID and set the meat and onions aside. Bring the liquid back to the boil, then continue to simmer until it is sticky and shiny. Put the meat back into the pan, stir well and season to taste.

TRANSFER EVERYTHING to an ovenproof dish and sprinkle with the breadcrumbs and grated Parmesan. Place under a preheated grill or in an oven preheated to 180°C/Fan 160°C/Gas mark 4, until the top is golden.

BEEF IN STOUT

This is a classic beef casserole, but you can spice it up with Worcestershire sauce or Tabasco if you like, or add some chopped chilli.

4 tbsp vegetable oil
300g baby onions
300g Chantenay carrots, cleaned and trimmed
500g beef chuck, cubed
4 tbsp plain flour
4 garlic cloves, chopped
2 x 440ml cans of stout
Worcestershire sauce
300g small button mushrooms
1 tbsp olive oil
2 tbsp chopped flatleaf parsley
salt and freshly ground black pepper

SERVES 4

HEAT 2 TABLESPOONS OF OIL in a large pan or casserole dish and gently cook the baby onions over a low heat until they are just golden. Remove the onions from the pan and set them aside. Add the Chantenay carrots and cook until golden, then set aside with the onions.

SEASON THE BEEF with salt and pepper and then toss in a bowl with the flour so that all the pieces are lightly coated. Add 2 tablespoons of fresh oil to the pan and turn up the heat. Brown the meat in batches, being careful not to overcrowd the pan. Once the meat is brown on all sides, put it back into the pan and add the onions, carrots and chopped garlic. Pour in the stout and cover the pan.

COOK OVER A LOW HEAT for 3 hours, or until the beef is tender. Once the meat is cooked through and soft, add a few drops of Worcestershire sauce and season to taste.

SAUTÉ THE MUSHROOMS in the olive oil until they are soft and nicely coloured and then add them to the stew. Sprinkle over the chopped parsley and serve.

BEEF STEW WITH BUTTERNUT SQUASH

My neighbours Karen and Stevie G made this one New Year's Eve and found that it works perfectly in a slow-cooker. Just put everything in and leave it.

600g beef chuck steak
50g plain flour
2 tbsp vegetable oil
1 butternut squash
2 small red onions,
    cut in half
2 garlic cloves, finely
    chopped
3–4 thyme sprigs, leaves
    picked from the stems
2 tbsp tomato purée
400ml Chicken stock
    (see page 282)
250g small new potatoes
splash of Worcestershire
    sauce
splash of balsamic vinegar
2 tbsp chopped flatleaf
    parsley
salt and freshly ground
    black pepper

SERVES 4

TRIM ANY EXCESS FAT and sinew from the beef with a sharp knife. Dice the meat into cubes of about 2.5cm. Season the cubes with salt and pepper, then toss them in a bowl with the plain flour.

HEAT THE OIL in a smoking-hot pan, then add the meat and colour it on all sides. Be careful not to overcrowd the pan or the meat will stew and not colour. Remove the beef from the pan and set it aside.

PEEL THE BUTTERNUT SQUASH and cut it into cubes of about the same size as the meat. Add the squash to the pan (in batches if necessary) and quickly brown on all sides. As the squash browns, remove it from the pan and set aside.

ADD THE RED ONIONS and chopped garlic to the pan together with the thyme leaves and cook for 10 minutes. Add the tomato purée and continue to cook for another 2–3 minutes. Put the meat back into the pan, pour in the chicken stock to cover, then put a lid on the pan. Leave to simmer for 1 hour and 15 minutes, then add the squash and the new potatoes to the pan and continue to cook for another 30 minutes.

FINISH with a splash of Worcestershire sauce and balsamic vinegar and season with salt and pepper to taste. Sprinkle over the chopped parsley and serve.

SEARED STEAK WITH ROCKET

It's useful to keep some of this parsley butter in the freezer, ready to use on steak and other dishes, such as Côte de boeuf (see page 160).

4 large Portobello
   mushrooms
olive oil
1 large shallot, sliced
4 thyme sprigs
60ml white wine
4 x 150g rib-eye steaks
1 bag of wild rocket leaves
balsamic vinegar
salt and freshly ground
   black pepper

For the parsley butter
2 garlic cloves, finely
   chopped
1 tbsp chopped flatleaf
   parsley
zest of 1 lemon
70g butter, at room
   temperature

SERVES 4

MAKE THE PARSLEY BUTTER. Mix the chopped garlic, parsley, lemon zest and butter together in a bowl. Place the mixture on a sheet of cling film and then roll it up to form a cylinder. Twist the ends of the cling film to keep the butter tightly packed and leave it in the fridge to chill for 1 hour.

PREHEAT THE OVEN to 180°C/Fan 160°C/Gas mark 4.

CLEAN THE MUSHROOMS with a damp cloth and place them in a roasting tin. Season the mushrooms with salt and pepper, drizzle over some olive oil and then add the sliced shallot, thyme and white wine. Cover the tin with a sheet of foil and bake in the preheated oven for 15–20 minutes. Remove the foil and continue cooking for about another 5 minutes until most (but not all) of the liquid has evaporated. Leave the oven on for finishing the steaks later

SEASON THE RIB-EYE STEAKS with salt and pepper and brush them with a little olive oil. Heat a griddle pan and cook the steaks for about 1 minute until grill lines have formed. Rotate the steaks and cook for another minute so that a second set of grill lines form, 'crossing' the first set. Turn the steaks over and repeat the cross grilling on the other side. If at this stage the meat is not cooked enough, finish it off in the oven. Once the steaks are cooked, set them aside to rest for 5 minutes.

WHEN READY TO SERVE, dice the parsley butter and place a few dice over the steaks. Place the steaks in the oven for 2–3 minutes, which should be just enough time to melt the butter and reheat the meat. Place a mushroom on each steak and spoon the shallot and white wine cooking juices over the meat. Serve with a fresh rocket salad, seasoned with olive oil and balsamic vinegar.

BEEF CHEEKS AND POLENTA

This always sells out when it's on the menu at the restaurant.
The meat should be so tender you can eat it with a spoon.

2 beef cheeks
4 tbsp olive oil
1 carrot, roughly chopped
1 onion, diced
½ head of garlic, chopped
1 celery stick, chopped
1 leek, chopped
4 thyme sprigs
12 black peppercorns
2 tbsp tomato purée
1 bottle of red wine
1 litre Chicken stock
  (see page 282)
splash of balsamic vinegar
splash of Worcestershire
  sauce
salt and freshly ground
  black pepper

For the polenta
200ml milk
200g coarse polenta
60g butter
50g Parmesan cheese,
  freshly grated

SERVES 4

TRIM the beef cheeks and remove as much sinew as possible.
Season with salt and pepper. Heat 2 tablespoons of oil in a heavy-
based pan and brown the cheeks on all sides. Remove and set aside.

TIP THE USED OIL out of the pan and add 2 tablespoons of fresh
oil. Add the carrot and once it starts to turn golden, add the
onion and garlic, then the celery and leek. Add the thyme and
peppercorns and mix everything together. When all the vegetables
are golden, add the tomato paste and cook for 2 minutes.

POUR IN THE RED WINE and stir, scraping up all the sticky bits
from the bottom of the pan, then cook until the liquid is reduced
and you have a sticky sauce – about 12–14 minutes.

PUT THE BEEF CHEEKS back into the pan and cover with the
chicken stock. Bring to the boil, skim the surface and cover with
a circle of greaseproof paper. Simmer over a low heat for 1½ hours
or until the meat is soft and almost falling apart. If you prefer, cook
the beef in the oven at 180°C/Fan 160°C/Gas mark 4 for 1½ hours.

ONCE THE CHEEKS ARE COOKED, take them out of the liquid and
set aside. Pass the liquid through a sieve, then pour into a pan and
reduce to a sauce-like consistency. This will take about 10 minutes.
Add a splash each of balsamic vinegar and Worcestershire sauce.
When the cheeks have cooled slightly, carve them into portions .

PREPARE THE POLENTA while the meat is cooking. Pour the milk
into a pan, add 800ml of water and bring the boil. Season and
then pour in the polenta while whisking. Simmer for 20 minutes,
continuing to whisk and stir regularly.

ONCE THE POLENTA IS COOKED and has started to come away from
the sides of the pan, add the butter and Parmesan and season to
taste. Pour the polenta onto plates, add the beef cheeks on top and
pour over the reduced cooking juices.

RACK OF LAMB WITH PISTACHIO CRUST

French trimming a rack of lamb simply means removing the excess
fat from the tops of the bones, but your butcher will do this for you.
The pistachio mixture freezes well so if you have any left,
pop it in the freezer for another time.

2 racks of lamb, French-
 trimmed (ask the butcher
 to do this for you)
2 tbsp olive oil
80g pistachio nuts
 (shelled weight)
80g Japanese panko
 breadcrumbs
Dijon mustard, for coating
 the lamb
salt and freshly ground
 black pepper

SERVES 4-6

PREHEAT THE OVEN to 180°C/Fan 160°C/Gas mark 4. Using a sharp
knife, remove any excess fat and sinew from the meat, as well as
the layer of fat from the top. Season the racks with salt and pepper.

HEAT THE OLIVE OIL in a frying pan and brown the racks until
they are golden on all sides.

TRANSFER THE LAMB from the pan to a roasting tin and wrap the
tips of the bones tightly with tin foil – this will stop them from
burning in the oven. Put the rack into the oven and cook for about
7 minutes, or until it is just warm in the centre when pricked with
a sharp knife. Once cooked, take the lamb out of the oven and set
it aside to rest. Turn the oven up to 200°C/Fan 180°C/Gas mark 6.

CRUSH THE PISTACHIOS in a blender. Because pistachios are oily,
they will eventually start to form a paste rather than a powder. At
this point, add the breadcrumbs and blend for a few more seconds
– this should bring it back to a smooth powder.

ONCE THE RACKS HAVE RESTED, cover them in a very thin layer
of mustard, then sprinkle the pistachio mixture over them – the
mustard should help it stick to the lamb. Finish by reheating the
lamb in the oven for about 5 minutes, or until the centre is hot
again and the crust is lightly toasted.

OLIVE-STUFFED LAMB

If you don't have a pan large enough for browning the meat, you can put it into the oven at maximum temperature for 7 minutes, then turn the oven down and finish the meat as below.

1 leg of lamb, boned or tunnel-boned (your butcher will do this for you)
2 tbsp anchovy paste
salsa verde (see page 160)
3 garlic cloves
100g pitted green olives
1 tbsp rosemary
grated zest of 2 lemons
100g wild garlic leaves or baby spinach
2–3 tbsp olive oil
salt and freshly ground black pepper

SERVES 4-6

OPEN THE LAMB OUT FLAT on a board so that it is ready to be rolled. Put the lamb between two layers of cling film and then flatten out the meat with something heavy, such as a frying pan or rolling pin.

MIX THE ANCHOVY PASTE with 2 tablespoons of the salsa verde and rub this onto the inside of the lamb leg. Roughly chop the garlic, green olives and rosemary and sprinkle all over the lamb. Add the lemon zest and season with salt and pepper, bearing in mind that the anchovies are already quite salty. Finally, lay the wild garlic or spinach leaves on top.

TIGHTLY ROLL THE LAMB LEG and tie with butchers' string in several places. It is best to let the lamb rest in the fridge overnight, but remember to take it out 1 hour before cooking so that the meat can come up to room temperature before you cook it.

PREHEAT THE OVEN to 180°C/Fan 160°C/Gas mark 4. Heat the olive oil in a frying pan and brown the meat on all sides. Transfer the meat to the preheated oven and cook for 35–40 minutes, depending on the size of the leg. When cooked, the meat should be just warm in the centre when pricked with a sharp knife.

REMOVE THE LAMB from the oven and leave to rest for 10–15 minutes before serving with rest of the salsa verde (see page 160).

SEARED LAMB WITH MINT AND FETA

You can also make this salad with leftover roast lamb.
Just slice the lamb and mix with the salad ingredients.

4 lamb rump steaks
4 tbsp olive oil, plus extra
    for dressing the salad
200g feta cheese, cut
    into cubes
1 red onion, finely sliced
1 tbsp pine nuts
2 tbsp chopped mint
2 tbsp chopped flatleaf
    parsley
2 tbsp chopped basil
1 bag of mixed salad leaves
aged balsamic vinegar,
    for serving
salt and freshly ground
    black pepper

SERVES 4

TRIM ANY EXCESS FAT from the steaks with a sharp knife and season them well. Preheat the oven to 180°C/Fan 160°C/Gas mark 4.

HEAT 4 TABLESPOONS OF OLIVE OIL in a frying pan and brown the lamb on all sides. Transfer the pan to the preheated oven and cook the lamb for about 4 minutes on each side. Remove from the oven and leave to rest in a warm place.

MIX THE FETA, onion and pine nuts with the chopped herbs and salad leaves. Add some olive oil and season with salt and pepper.

CARVE THE LAMB STEAKS into two or three slices and mix with the salad. Finish with a few drops of balsamic vinegar and serve immediately.

BRAISED NECKS OF LAMB

Lamb necks are a smaller, tastier alternative to lamb shanks. I first started to cook them when I was at the Connaught and they were always a great seller. Use any leftovers from this dish as a pasta sauce.

2 tbsp groundnut oil
4 necks of lamb
2 carrots, chopped
1 celery stick, chopped
1 head of garlic, cut in half
2 medium onions, chopped
5 white peppercorns, crushed
1 thyme sprig
1 bay leaf
1 tbsp tomato purée
150ml white wine
1–1½ litres Chicken stock (see page 282)
1 tbsp chopped flatleaf parsley
salt and freshly ground black pepper

SERVES 4

YOU NEED AN OVENPROOF PAN or casserole dish large enough to hold the necks and all the vegetables. Heat the oil in the pan and colour the lamb necks until golden brown. Remove them, then add the vegetables, spices and herbs and brown gently.

PREHEAT THE OVEN to 160°C/Fan 140°C/Gas mark 3.

PUT THE LAMB NECKS BACK INTO THE PAN, add the tomato purée and cook for 2 minutes. Pour in the white wine and stir to scrape up all the sticky bits from the bottom of the pan, then add enough stock to cover.

BRING THE STOCK BACK TO THE BOIL, season, and cover with a circle of parchment paper. Cook in the preheated oven for 2½ hours. Check the seasoning and add the chopped parsley just before serving.

SERVE WITH SOME POLENTA OR MASH to soak up the juices and perhaps some seasonal cabbage.

CITRUS-BRAISED NECK OF LAMB

This is fantastic served with some couscous to absorb the tasty juices.

800g lamb neck fillets
2 tbsp olive oil
1 large onion, chopped
2 oranges
1 lemon
50ml sweet Madeira
500ml Chicken stock
  (see page 282)
100g broad beans
  (shelled weight)
50g butter
150g cherry tomatoes,
  halved
1 tbsp chopped mint
1 tbsp chopped coriander
salt and freshly ground
  black pepper

SERVES 4

TRIM ANY EXCESS FAT and sinew from the meat with a sharp knife, then season. Heat the olive oil in a pan and brown the fillets on all sides. Remove the fillets and set them aside. Add the chopped onion and cook gently until it is soft but not coloured.

GRATE THE ZEST of the oranges and half the lemon and add to the pan. Pour in the Madeira and stir, scraping up all the sticky bits from the bottom of the pan. Put the neck fillets back into the pan and pour in the stock. Cover with a circle of greaseproof paper and simmer for 1¼ hours or until the meat is soft.

PEEL the oranges and lemon and divide them into segments. Blanch the broad beans in boiling water for 1–2 minutes.

REMOVE THE LAMB FILLETS from the pan and set them aside. Put the pan with the cooking liquid and onions back on a high heat for 4–5 minutes until the liquid has reduced and has a soup-like consistency. Add the butter, bring back to the boil and whisk vigorously to thicken the sauce.

ADD THE FRUIT SEGMENTS, halved cherry tomatoes and herbs. Put the lamb and beans back into the pan to warm through briefly, then serve.

SLOW-COOKED LAMB SHOULDER

This is very easy to prepare, then you can forget about it while it cooks away for hours.

1 x 1.75kg lamb shoulder
1 head of garlic, split into cloves
a few rosemary sprigs
knob of butter, for greasing the dish
2 onions, thinly sliced
4 large potatoes, thinly sliced
1 thyme sprig
700ml–1 litre Chicken stock (see page 282)
salt and freshly ground black pepper

SERVES 4

MAKE SMALL INCISIONS all over the lamb shoulder with a sharp knife. Push a clove of garlic and a few rosemary leaves into each incision. Season the lamb. Preheat the oven to 140°C/ Fan 120°C/ Gas mark 1.

BUTTER THE BASE of a large ovenproof dish and add a layer of sliced onions. Add a layer of sliced potatoes, sprinkle with thyme and season. Repeat the layers until the potatoes and onions are used up, then place the lamb shoulder on top.

POUR OVER THE CHICKEN STOCK – you need enough to cover and moisten the potatoes but not saturate them. Bake in the preheated oven for 4 hours, until the lamb is falling off the bone.

LET EVERYONE HELP THEMSELVES to big spoonfuls of melting lamb and vegetables.

LANCASHIRE HOT POT

You can use little chops for this instead of lamb shoulder if you prefer.

4 tbsp vegetable oil
2 large onions, chopped
2 garlic cloves, finely
   chopped
2 large carrots, diced
500g lamb shoulder, diced
4 tbsp plain flour
6 lamb's kidneys, diced
2 bay leaves
4 thyme sprigs
200ml Chicken stock
   (see page 282)
Worcestershire sauce
500g medium-sized potatoes
knob of butter
salt and freshly ground
   black pepper

SERVES 4

HEAT THE OIL in a large saucepan and gently cook the onions and garlic over a low heat until soft. Remove from the pan, turn up the heat and quickly brown the diced carrots. Set them aside with the onions.

SEASON THE LAMB with salt and pepper and then toss in a bowl with the flour so that all the pieces are lightly coated. Add some fresh oil to the pan and turn up the heat. Brown the meat in batches, taking care not to overcrowd the pan or the meat will stew and not colour. Brown the kidneys in the same way.

PUT ALL THE MEAT back into the pan and add the cooked vegetables and the bay leaves and thyme. Cover with the chicken stock, bring to the boil, then add a few drops of Worcestershire sauce and season with salt and pepper to taste. Remove the bay leaves, then spoon the stew into a large ovenproof dish.

PREHEAT THE OVEN to 180°C/Fan 160°C/Gas mark 4. Peel the potatoes and slice them into discs 0.5 cm−1cm thick. Arrange these potato slices over the stew and add the butter and some salt on top.

COVER THE DISH WITH FOIL and place it on a baking sheet, then cook in the preheated oven for 90 minutes. Remove the foil and cook for another 20−25 minutes until the potato topping is golden.

IRISH STEW

Mutton is generally agreed to be meat from sheep that are over two years old. Once hard to find, mutton is reappearing in butchers' shops, but if you can't find any you can use lamb instead.

2 tbsp vegetable oil
500g mutton shoulder, diced
2 large onions, diced
2 garlic cloves, chopped
800ml Chicken stock (see page 282))
2–3 thyme sprigs
1 bay leaf
2 large carrots, diced
300g new potatoes, halved
2 tbsp chopped flatleaf parsley
salt and freshly ground black pepper

SERVES 4-6

HEAT THE OIL in a heavy-based pan. Season the diced mutton and colour it in the pan for a few minutes – you will need to do this in batches so you don't overcrowd the pan.

WHEN THE MUTTON IS BROWNED, set it aside and gently cook the onions and garlic for 5–6 minutes.

PUT EVERYTHING BACK IN THE PAN and add the chicken stock, thyme and bay leaf and top up with boiling water to cover. Bring the stew back to the boil and simmer for 2 hours. Remove any scum from the surface with a spoon from time to time.

AFTER 90 MINUTES, check the seasoning and add more salt if needed. Add the carrots and potatoes to the pan for the remaining 30 minutes and cover with a circle of greaseproof paper. Finally, add the chopped parsley and serve.

LAMBS' KIDNEYS WITH BUTTER BEANS

I've never been a great offal fan, but I do like the delicate flavour of lambs' kidneys. The secret is not to overcook them – leave them slightly pink in the middle. Ask your butcher to trim the kidneys for you and remove any excess sinew.

5 tbsp olive oil
1 small onion, diced
2 garlic cloves, crushed
75g pancetta
1 tbsp capers
1 x 400g can of butter beans, drained and rinsed
1 tbsp sherry vinegar
8–12 lambs' kidneys, trimmed and ready to cook
2 tbsp plain flour
2 tbsp chopped flatleaf parsley
salt and freshly ground black pepper

SERVES 4

HEAT 1 TABLESPOON OF OIL in a frying pan and cook the onion and garlic until translucent. Add the pancetta and cook for another couple of minutes, then add the capers and butter beans and warm them through. Finish with the sherry vinegar and 2 tablespooons of olive oil, then set aside while you cook the kidneys.

SEASON THE KIDNEYS and dust them with flour. Heat the rest of the oil in a pan and sauté the kidneys until golden and crispy on both sides.

SPOON THE BEANS INTO A SERVING BOWL and add the kidneys on top. Sprinkle with the chopped parsley and serve immediately.

LIVER, BACON AND SAGE

Some foods make a perfect combination and liver, bacon and sage are a good example. Calves' liver is slightly more tender than lambs' liver but it is also more expensive. Both work well in this dish.

600g lambs' or calves' liver, cut into thin slices (your butcher will do this for you)
plain flour, for dusting
3 tbsp vegetable oil
100g dry-cured smoked streaky bacon, cut into fine strips
1 onion, sliced
8 sage leaves, chopped
splash of sherry vinegar
salt and freshly ground black pepper

SERVES 4–6

SEASON THE SLICES OF LIVER and coat them in plain flour. Heat 2 tablespoons of the oil in a heavy-based frying pan and cook the liver for about 1½ minutes on each side until lightly coloured. Remove from the pan and set aside to rest.

TIP THE OLD OIL out of the pan and add a tablespoon of fresh oil. Add the finely sliced bacon strips and fry over a medium heat for 2–3 minutes until the fat starts to run.

ADD THE SLICED ONION and cook over a high heat for 5–6 minutes until soft. Put the liver back into the pan and toss everything together. Add the sage and the sherry vinegar, check the seasoning and serve.

FISH
AND
SHELLFISH

PRAWNS AND ROMESCO

If possible, prepare the peppers a couple of days ahead so that they are really dry. If you have some romesco left over, store it in the freezer. It's good served with pork and lamb as well as fish.

8 slices of baguette
4 tbsp olive oil
600g raw prawns, peeled
splash of white wine
small handful of chives
    and flatleaf parsley,
    finely chopped

For the romesco
1 x 290g jar of cooked
    red peppers
2 tbsp chopped fresh
    rosemary
2 garlic cloves, finely
    chopped
50g flaked almonds
50g dry white breadcrumbs
1–2 tbsp olive oil
salt and freshly ground
    black pepper

SERVES 4

START THE ROMESCO the day before you want to cook this dish. Drain the oil from the peppers and pat them dry with kitchen paper to remove any excess moisture. Lay the peppers on a baking sheet, then sprinkle over the chopped rosemary and garlic, and season with salt and pepper. Leave the baking sheet in the kitchen so the peppers dry out slightly.

PREHEAT YOUR OVEN to 150°C/Fan 130°C/Gas mark 2. Spread out the flaked almonds on a baking sheet and put them in the oven for about 5 minutes. Watch that they don't burn. When they are toasted, remove and leave them to cool down. Put the cooled almonds in a food processor with the dried peppers, breadcrumbs and enough olive oil to blend to a sandy paste. Check the seasoning.

BRUSH THE SLICES OF BAGUETTE with 2 tablespoons of the olive oil and season with salt and pepper. Cook on a hot griddle for 1–2 minutes each side until golden.

HEAT THE REMAINING OIL in a pan and fry the prawns for 3–4 minutes, tossing frequently until they turn pink. When the prawns are almost cooked, add a splash of white wine and let that evaporate, then add the romesco, mixing well to ensure all the prawns are coated. Add the chopped chives and parsley and continue to cook for a further 1–2 minutes. Spoon the prawns onto the grilled slices of baguette.

STIR-FRIED NOODLES WITH SHRIMP

6 dried Chinese mushrooms
2 tbsp sesame oil
1 onion, chopped finely
50g chopped pancetta
1 tsp finely chopped
   root ginger
2 tsp Madras curry powder
1 heaped tbsp brown shrimp
200ml Chicken stock
   (see page 282)
200g rice noodles
100g cooked chicken,
   shredded
salt and freshly ground
   black pepper

SERVES 4

PUT THE DRIED MUSHROOMS in warm water and leave to soak for 30 minutes. Drain and set aside.

HEAT THE SESAME OIL in a pan and sauté the onion, pancetta and ginger until softened. Add the curry powder and cook for a few minutes longer, then add the shrimp. Take the pan off the heat and set aside.

HEAT THE CHICKEN STOCK in a separate pan. Add the noodles, then the chicken and drained mushrooms and bring to the boil. Add the shrimp mixture to the noodles, season, and toss everything together. Serve immediately.

PRAWN CURRY

2 x 400ml cans of coconut
   milk
800g raw prawns, shelled
   and cleaned
1 mango (Alphonso are
   the best), flesh diced
1 tbsp chopped coriander
2 tbsp chopped Thai basil

For the curry paste
2 red chillies, seeded
zest and juice of 1 lime
2 lemon grass stems
1 tbsp chopped ginger
4 garlic cloves, chopped
1 small onion, diced

SERVES 4

POUR THE COCONUT MILK into a pan and boil until it is reduced by half.

PUT THE CURRY PASTE ingredients into a blender and blitz until smooth.

ADD THE PASTE AND SHELLED PRAWNS to the pan of coconut milk and bring to a simmer. Cook for 5 minutes until prawns are done, then add the mango. Add the chopped coriander and Thai basil before serving.

PRAWNS AND PIPERADE

Make the piperade the day before. It tastes even better when all the flavours have had time to mingle.

600g raw prawns, peeled
2 tbsp olive oil, plus extra for brushing the sourdough
2 tbsp white wine
2 tbsp chopped flatleaf parsley
4 large slices of sourdough bread

For the piperade
6 medium tomatoes
2 red peppers
1 yellow pepper
2 tbsp olive oil
50g Parma ham, thinly sliced
1 medium onion, sliced
2 garlic cloves, finely chopped
1 red chilli, seeded and finely chopped
1 fennel bulb, chopped
splash of sherry vinegar
2 tbsp chopped chives
salt and freshly ground black pepper

SERVES 4

TO MAKE THE PIPERADE, cut the tomatoes lengthwise into 4 pieces. Scoop out the centres, then cut each piece in half again. Cut the peppers into quarters and remove the seeds and white flesh inside. Cut the pepper quarters into strips roughly the same size as the tomatoes.

HEAT TWO TABLESPOONS OF OLIVE OIL in a large frying pan, add the Parma ham slices and cook for about 30 seconds. Add the onion and garlic to the pan and continue to cook for 4–5 minutes until the onion is soft.

ADD THE CHOPPED CHILLI, peppers and fennel and cook over a medium heat for around 20 minutes, or until the peppers and fennel have softened. Finally add the tomato slices, a splash of sherry vinegar and the chopped chives, then season with salt and pepper. Mix everything together well and cook for another 1–2 minutes.

SEASON THE PRAWNS with salt and pepper. Heat 2 tablespoons of olive oil in a large frying pan and fry the prawns for 3–4 minutes, turning them frequently until they have turned pink and are cooked through. Add the white wine and parsley to the pan towards the end of the cooking time.

BRUSH THE SLICES OF SOURDOUGH with oil and grill them on a hot griddle until golden.

SPOON SOME PIPERADE onto each slice of toast and then add the prawns on top.

SPICY SQUID AND RED PEPPER STEW

There's nothing worse than rubbery squid
so make sure you don't overcook it.

500g squid, cleaned
(ask your fishmonger
to do this for you)
4 tbsp olive oil
2 shallots, peeled and sliced
2 garlic cloves, chopped
1 red chilli, seeded and
finely chopped
splash of sherry vinegar
2 red peppers
2 yellow peppers
1 x 400g can of plum
tomatoes
small handful of fresh
basil leaves, chopped
2 tbsp chopped flatleaf
parsley
grated zest and juice
of 1 lime
1 baguette, sliced
salt and freshly ground
black pepper

SERVES 4

CUT THE SQUID into equal-sized pieces about 2cm square.
Slice the tentacles into bite-sized pieces and set aside.

HEAT 2 TABLESPOONS OF OLIVE OIL in a large pan, add the
shallots and cook for 2–3 minutes over a medium heat. Add
the chopped garlic and chilli and continue to cook for another
couple of minutes, then add a splash of sherry vinegar.

CUT EACH PEPPER into 4 and remove the seeds and white flesh
inside. Dice the peppers into 2cm pieces, add these to the
shallots and cook for 5–6 minutes. Roughly chop the canned
tomatoes and add them to the stew. Continue to cook for
another 20 minutes, until the stew starts to thicken up.

HEAT THE REST OF THE OLIVE OIL in a frying pan and fry the
squid for about 2 minutes. You'll need to do this in batches so you
don't overcrowd the pan and stew the squid instead of sautéing it.

ADD THE SQUID TO THE STEW, along with the chopped basil and
parsley, and mix well. Add the lime zest and juice, cook for another
2 minutes, then season to taste.

GRILL THE SLICES of baguette and serve with the squid and
pepper stew.

SQUID WITH WHITE BEAN AND TREVISO SALAD

Treviso – Italian chicory – is best for this but you can use radicchio instead.

1 head of Treviso chicory
60g Parmesan shavings
1 x 400g can of haricot
    beans, drained
2 celery sticks, finely diced
small handful of flatleaf
    parsley, chopped
500g squid, cleaned
    (your fishmonger
    will do this for you)
vegetable oil, for deep-frying
plain flour, for dusting
pinch of cayenne
squeeze of lemon juice,
    for serving
olive oil, for serving
salt and freshly ground
    black pepper

SERVES 4

SEPARATE THE LEAVES of the chicory and chop them into similar-sized pieces. Take care not to bruise the leaves. Place the chopped leaves in a large bowl and add the Parmesan shavings, beans, diced celery and parsley. Season to taste and toss everything together.

CUT THE SQUID, body and tentacles, into bite-sized pieces, then season with salt and pepper. Half-fill a large pan with vegetable oil and bring to a temperature of 180°C.

DREDGE THE SQUID with flour, shake off the excess and deep-fry for 1–2 minutes until golden – you will need to cook the squid in batches so you don't overcrowd the pan. Drain each batch of squid on kitchen paper, then sprinkle with cayenne and seasoning.

ADD THE DEEP-FRIED SQUID to the salad and mix gently. Add a squeeze of lemon juice and a drizzle of olive oil before serving.

GRILLED SQUID AND TOMATO SALSA

This is great for a barbecue. Once the salsa is made,
all you have to do is throw the squid on the grill.

6–8 baby squid, depending
   on size, cleaned
1 tbsp olive oil
salt and freshly ground
   black pepper

For the tomato salsa
1 avocado
200g cherry tomatoes,
   cut in half
1 tbsp chopped basil
1 tbsp chopped coriander
1 tbsp olive oil
1 tbsp red wine vinegar
1 tbsp finely chopped
   red onion

SERVES 4

BRUSH THE SQUID WITH OIL, then season. Heat a griddle pan
and grill the squid briefly on both sides.

MIX ALL THE SALSA ingredients in a bowl and season to taste.

SERVE the grilled squid with the salsa.

BASQUE FISH SOUP

This is a very adaptable recipe. Use cod, pollock or whatever
you can find and increase the shellfish if you like.

750g mixed fish and
shellfish: monkfish,
squid raw prawns
1 tbsp olive oil
1 onion, chopped
3 garlic cloves, chopped
1 rosemary sprig
1 thyme sprig
1 x 400g can of chopped
tomatoes
150ml red wine
500ml Fish stock
(see page 283)
1 tbsp basil
1 tbsp chopped flatleaf
parsley
salt and freshly ground
black pepper

SERVES 4

CUT THE MONKFISH into large 2cm dice and the squid into rings.
Peel the prawns.

HEAT THE OLIVE OIL in a large pan and sauté the onion, garlic,
rosemary and thyme until soft. Stir in the tomatoes and red wine,
then pour in the fish stock and bring to the boil. Add the monkfish
and seasoning, cover the pan and simmer for 5 minutes.

ADD THE SQUID AND PRAWNS just before serving and cook until
the prawns turn pink. Finish with fresh basil and parsley.

MUSSELS IN CURRY AND TOMATO SAUCE

I love this way of serving mussels. I had some curried mussel soup
in Scotland recently and thought curry and mussels a perfect combo.

1kg mussels in their shells
1–2 tbsp olive oil
3 large shallots, sliced
2 garlic cloves, finely
   chopped
2 tbsp mild curry powder
500ml white wine
200g Basic tomato sauce
   (see page 282) or tomato
   passata
250g cherry tomatoes,
   cut into quarters
1 lime, cut into quarters
150ml double cream
small handful of flatleaf
   parsley, chopped
salt and freshly ground
   black pepper

SERVES 4

CLEAN THE MUSSELS under cold running water, scrubbing the
shells well and removing the hairy beards. Discard any mussels
that are already open.

HEAT THE OLIVE OIL in a pan large enough to fit all the mussels,
then add the shallots and garlic. Cook for 1–2 minutes on a gentle
heat, add the curry powder and cook for another 2 minutes until
the shallots are nicely softened.

ADD THE WHITE WINE and the tomato sauce to the pan and bring
to the boil. Cook for 10 minutes or until the sauce starts to thicken.
Add the quartered tomatoes and lime wedges, then season with
salt and pepper.

TURN UP THE HEAT, add all the mussels and mix them carefully.
Cover the pan with a lid and cook for about 5 minutes, or until all
the mussels have opened.

ADD THE CREAM and bring back to the boil. Just before serving,
add the chopped parsley. Spoon into large bowls to serve, taking
care to discard any unopened mussels.

STEAMED MUSSELS IN CIDER

White wine is the classic with mussels but I like the different taste of the cider in this recipe. Always try to cook mussels on the day you buy them so they are as fresh as possible.

1kg mussels in their shells
1–2 tbsp olive oil
3 large shallots, sliced
½ head of garlic, sliced
   horizontally
1 lemon grass stem, crushed
   and cut into pieces
1 red chilli, seeded and
   chopped
1 lime, cut into quarters
500ml cider
150ml double cream
small handful of fresh
   coriander, chopped
salt and freshly ground
   black pepper

SERVES 4

CLEAN THE MUSSELS under cold running water, scrubbing the shells well and removing the hairy beards. Discard any mussels that are already open.

HEAT THE OLIVE OIL in a pan large enough to fit all the mussels. Add the shallots, garlic and lemon grass. Cook for 2–3 minutes on a medium heat, then add the chopped chilli and cook for another minute. Add the lime quarters to the pan.

ADD ALL THE MUSSELS and stir them carefully. Pour in the cider and cover the pan with a lid. Cook over a high heat for approximately 5 minutes, or until all the mussels have opened.

ADD THE CREAM and bring the liquid back to the boil. Season with salt and pepper, then spoon into large bowls, taking care to discard any unopened mussels. Sprinkle with chopped coriander before serving.

GRILLED SARDINES WITH EGG GRIBICHE

I love sardines and I love egg mayonnaise, but when one of my chefs came up with this combination I didn't think it would work. I was wrong – it's delicious.

4 slices of foccacia
2 tbsp olive oil
6 large sardines, filleted
   and pin-boned
mixed green salad leaves

For the gribiche
2 eggs
20ml white wine vinegar
1 tsp English mustard
40ml olive oil
80ml vegetable oil
3 tbsp Lilliput capers
3 tbsp chopped cornichons
small handful of flatleaf
   parsley, chopped
salt and freshly ground
   black pepper

SERVES 4

FIRST MAKE THE GRIBICHE. To hard-boil the eggs, put them in a pan of cold water, bring to the boil and boil for 7 minutes. Cool the eggs under cold running water, then peel off the shells. Separate the egg yolks from the whites. Place the egg yolks in a bowl and work them together into a paste. Chop the egg whites and set them aside.

ADD THE VINEGAR AND MUSTARD to the egg yolks and mix well. Slowly add the olive and vegetable oils while mixing, as if making mayonnaise. Add the rest of the gribiche ingredients, including the chopped egg whites, and mix together. Season with salt and pepper.

RUB THE FOCACCIA SLICES with olive oil and season with salt and pepper. Place them on a hot griddle and toast for 1–2 minutes on each side, until golden.

COOK THE SARDINES on the griddle for about 2 minutes on each side, then place them on the toasts. Add a spoonful of the gribiche on top and serve with a simple green salad.

TROUT WITH BEURRE NOISETTE, SPINACH AND PINE NUTS

Trout is an underused fish and a good, cheap alternative to salmon.

2 tbsp olive oil
4 trout fillets, skin on
100g butter
25g pine nuts
25g capers
250g spinach
salt and freshly ground
    black pepper

SERVES 4

HEAT THE OLIVE OIL in a large frying pan. Add the trout, skin-side down, and fry for about 2 minutes, until the skin is crispy. Turn and sear the trout on the other side, then remove from the pan.

ADD THE BUTTER to the pan and heat until it starts to foam and turn golden brown. Add the pine nuts and capers, then the spinach and cook until the spinach has wilted. Season with salt and pepper.

SERVE the spinach mixture onto plates and add the trout on top.

GRILLED TUNA WITH RED ONION SALAD

If you don't want to use tuna, monkfish also works well in this recipe.

2 large heads of chicory
2 small red onions,
    very thinly sliced
100g goats' cheese, diced
2 tbsp maple syrup
2 tbsp balsamic vinegar
2 tbsp Cabernet Sauvignon
    vinegar
120ml olive oil, plus extra
    for drizzling on the tuna
4 x 130g tuna steaks
small handful of fresh
    oregano, chopped
salt and freshly ground
    black pepper

SERVES 4

CUT THE HEADS OF CHICORY in half, remove the cores, then separate the leaves and slice them. In a large bowl, mix the chicory with the sliced red onions and goats' cheese.

IN A SEPARATE BOWL, mix the maple syrup with the balsamic and Cabernet Sauvignon vinegars. Season with a little salt and pepper, then gradually whisk in the olive oil.

DRIZZLE SOME OLIVE OIL over each tuna steak, and season them with salt and pepper. Heat a griddle pan and grill the tuna for 2–3 minutes on each side – tuna is best eaten rare.

ADD THE CHOPPED OREGANO and maple syrup vinaigrette to the salad, mix well and serve with the tuna steaks.

GRILLED SALMON WITH COURGETTE AND TOMATO SALAD

Scottish salmon is the best in the world, but only use it when it's in season and at its peak.

3 baby courgettes
½ cucumber
250g cherry tomatoes, halved
2 shallots, sliced into thin rings
2–3 tbsp chopped fresh basil
4 salmon steaks, skin on
olive oil, for brushing the salmon
salt and freshly ground black pepper

For the vinaigrette
1 tsp Dijon mustard
2 tbsp cider vinegar
80ml olive oil
salt and freshly ground black pepper

SERVES 4

FIRST MAKE THE SALAD. Slice the courgettes into thin discs. Cut the cucumber in half and slice thinly so you have half-moon shaped pieces. Mix the courgettes and cucumbers with the tomatoes, shallots and chopped basil in a bowl and season with salt and pepper.

SEASON THE SALMON STEAKS and brush them with olive oil. Cook them on a hot griddle pan for 3–4 minutes on each side, then set aside to rest for 2 minutes.

TO MAKE THE VINAIGRETTE, whisk the Dijon mustard, cider vinegar and seasoning together in a bowl, then gradually whisk in the olive oil. Dress the salad with the vinaigrette and serve with the salmon.

SALMON AND SPROUTING BROCCOLI SALAD

This is a lovely fresh summer salad. The broccoli and crunchy radishes go well with the salmon and make a welcome change from the usual salmon and mayo combination.

1 tbsp olive oil
300g salmon fillet
200g sprouting broccoli
8 small salad radishes, sliced
3 tbsp Classic vinaigrette
    (see page 282)
fresh mint leaves
salt and freshly ground
    black pepper

SERVES 4

HEAT THE OLIVE OIL in a frying pan. Season the salmon fillets on both sides with salt and pepper, then cook them in the pan for 2 minutes on each side, depending on the thickness. Remove from the pan and set aside to cool.

BRING A PAN OF SALTED WATER to the boil and blanch the broccoli until just cooked. Refresh in cold water, drain and set aside.

TO SERVE, cut the broccoli into pieces and put them in a bowl. Break up the salmon and add it to the bowl with the radishes. Finish with the vinaigrette and mint leaves, season and serve.

GRILLED SALMON WITH PAK CHOI AND GINGER

Ginger and salmon is a classic marriage of flavours. Use spring or summer cabbage if you like, instead of pak choi.

1 tbsp olive oil
4 salmon steaks, skin on
1 tbsp sesame oil
1 tsp chopped ginger
½ red chilli, seeded
    and finely chopped
3 pak choi
4 tbsp soy sauce
4 tbsp rice wine
salt and freshly ground
    black pepper

SERVES 4

HEAT A FRYING PAN and add the olive oil. Place the salmon steaks into the pan, skin-side down, and shake the pan gently. Cook the fish for 2½ minutes on each side, or until warm in the centre, then remove from the pan and set aside.

ADD THE SESAME OIL to the pan, then add the ginger and chilli and sauté briefly. Add the pak choi and sauté for 3 minutes.

POUR IN THE SOY SAUCE and rice wine and stir well, scraping up all the sticky bits from the bottom of the pan. Season. Serve immediately with the salmon steaks on top.

SALMON STEAKS WITH DILL CREAM

For this dish, ask your fishmonger for salmon steaks cut from a whole salmon. Each steak will have the spine through the centre, as well as the fillets from both sides.

2 large leeks
1 tbsp olive oil, plus extra
    for brushing the leeks
splash of white wine
3–4 thyme sprigs
1 garlic clove, crushed
    and skin on
4 salmon steaks, skin on
salt and freshly ground
    black pepper

For the dill cream
6 tbsp crème fraîche
1 lemon
small bunch of dill, chopped

SERVES 4

PREHEAT THE OVEN to 180°C/Fan 160°C/Gas mark 4. Peel away the outer layers of the leeks, then wash and dry them well. Cut each leek into 4 chunks, brush with olive oil and grill them on a hot griddle pan for 1–2 minutes.

PLACE THE LEEKS on a baking sheet lined with baking parchment, then add a splash of wine, thyme, garlic and some salt and pepper. Cover with foil and bake in the preheated oven for 15–20 minutes.

HEAT THE OLIVE OIL in a frying pan. Season the salmon steaks on both sides with salt and pepper, then cook them in the pan for 3 minutes on each side. Once the steaks are cooked, remove them from the pan and set aside to rest for a couple of minutes.

TO MAKE THE DILL CREAM, mix the crème fraîche with the zest of the lemon and a squeeze of juice. Add the chopped dill, season with salt and pepper and mix well.

SERVE THE SALMON with a couple of pieces of leek on each plate and add a big dollop of dill cream. Finish with a squeeze of lemon juice and serve at once.

SALMON WITH SPICY RICE NOODLES

Don't overcook the salmon during the first stage in the pan.
It'll carry on cooking in the broth.

1 tbsp sesame oil
1 garlic clove, sliced
1 red chilli, seeded
    and sliced
50g button mushrooms,
    sliced
4 baby sweetcorn, each
    cut into 3 pieces
200ml Vegetable stock
    (see page 283)
4 salmon steaks, skinned
150g precooked rice noodles
1 tbsp chopped chives
1 tbsp chopped coriander
4 spring onions, chopped
handful of spinach leaves,
    stalks removed
salt and freshly ground
    black pepper

SERVES 4

HEAT THE SESAME OIL in a deep frying pan and sauté the garlic, chilli, mushrooms and baby sweetcorn. Add the vegetable stock and bring to the boil, then leave to one side.

FRY THE FISH, skin-side down, in a shallow pan for 2 minutes on each side until just cooked.

BRING THE BROTH BACK UP TO THE BOIL, add the noodles, fresh herbs, spring onions and spinach. Season to taste.

SERVE in large bowls with the salmon placed on top.

COD TAGINE WITH CHICKPEAS

The recipe makes more harissa than you need for this dish, but it can be stored in the fridge for a month or so and works well with meat as well as fish.

2 tbsp olive oil
1 large carrot, diced
1 large red onion, diced
2 garlic cloves, crushed
½ tsp ground turmeric
small knob of fresh
    ginger, chopped
2 tbsp white wine
250ml Chicken stock
    (see page 282) or water
125g cherry tomatoes,
    cut in half
100g sultanas, soaked
    in warm water for
    10 minutes
1 x 400g can of chickpeas,
    drained
zest of 1 lemon
4 x 130g cod fillets, skin on
salt and freshly ground
    black pepper

For the harissa paste
1 tbsp tomato purée
1 tbsp harissa
1 garlic clove, crushed
juice of ½ lemon
1 tsp paprika
1 tsp cumin powder
2 tbsp olive oil
1 tbsp chopped coriander

SERVES 4

TO MAKE THE HARISSA, mix all the ingredients together in a bowl and stir well until everything is combined. Leave to one side.

HEAT 1 TABLESPOON OF OLIVE OIL in a large frying pan, then add the carrot, onion and crushed garlic. Cook the vegetables over a medium heat for 4–5 minutes, then add the turmeric and chopped ginger to the pan. Continue to cook for 3–4 minutes, then add the white wine and season with salt. Let the wine reduce, then add the chicken stock or water and bring to the boil.

ADD THE CHERRY TOMATOES, sultanas, chickpeas, lemon zest and 1 heaped tablespoon of the harissa. Mix everything together well, turn the heat down a little and cook for another 10–15 minutes.

PREHEAT THE OVEN to 180°C/Fan 160°C/Gas mark 4. Season the cod on all sides with salt and pepper. Heat 1 tablespoon of olive oil in a frying pan and brown the cod, skin-side down, for 2 minutes. Remove the fillets from the pan, place them on a baking sheet and cook in the preheated oven for 4 minutes – thick fillets may take a little longer.

TO SERVE, spoon the chickpea mixture onto serving plates and place the cod on top.

SALT COD GRATIN

I love salt cod and always cook it at Christmas.
Make sure you allow enough time to soak it properly.

500g salt cod
2 garlic cloves
2–3 thyme sprigs
1 bay leaf
600ml milk
3 medium potatoes
knob of butter
1 onion, diced
2 lemons
2 tbsp chopped flatleaf
    parsley
50g pine nuts
50g Japanese panko
    breadcrumbs or ordinary
    breadcrumbs
50g Parmesan cheese,
    freshly grated
olive oil, for drizzling
salt and freshly ground
    black pepper

SERVES 4

TO PREPARE THE SALT COD, soak the fish in plenty of cold water overnight, then drain. Change the water at least once during the soaking process. Put the cod in a pan with the garlic, thyme and bay leaf. Pour in the milk to cover and bring to a simmer.

POACH THE COD for 8–10 minutes until the fish is soft and breaks apart. Remove the cod from the pan, then strain the milk and set it aside for cooking the potatoes. Separate the fish from the skin and bones, keeping only the flesh and discarding the rest. Set aside.

PEEL THE POTATOES and cut them into equal-sized pieces. Cover the potatoes with the strained cooking milk, topping it up with water if necessary. Taste the cooking liquid and season with salt and pepper if needed. Simmer very slowly for 12–14 minutes until the potatoes are just cooked.

DRAIN THE MILK from the pan and work the potatoes with a spatula to break them up. Add the cooked cod, gently folding it into the potato and making sure not to mush it up too much.

HEAT A KNOB OF BUTTER in a frying pan and cook the diced onion for 4–5 minutes until soft and golden. Add the onion to the cod and potato and mix well. Add the juice of half a lemon and the chopped parsley, then season with salt and pepper. Put the mixture into four ramekins and leave to one side.

PREHEAT THE OVEN to 180°C/Fan 160°C/Gas mark 4. Put the pine nuts in a dry frying pan and place the pan over a medium heat. Keep tossing the pine nuts until they are golden – watch them carefully so they don't burn. Let them cool slightly.

BLITZ THE BREADCRUMBS and cooled pine nuts in a food processor with the grated zest of both the lemons. Sprinkle the breadcrumb mixture over the ramekins, add the grated Parmesan and drizzle with a little olive oil. Place the ramekins on a baking tray and bake in the oven for 20–25 minutes.

POACHED COD AND LENTILS

If possible, use French Puy lentils or Italian Castelluccio lentils for the best flavour – not the little red ones. You could also make this with butter beans or chickpeas.

45g butter
1 tbsp olive oil
1 large white onion, diced
1 garlic clove, finely chopped
100g pancetta, chopped
200g Puy lentils
splash of white wine
600ml Chicken stock (see page 282)
4 x 130g cod fillets, skinned and trimmed
2 handfuls of baby spinach leaves
4 spring onions, chopped
2 tbsp chopped flatleaf parsley
salt and freshly ground black pepper

For the poaching liquid
300ml white wine
1 star anise
¼ tsp fennel seeds
5 coriander seeds
1 thyme sprig
a few basil leaves
juice of ½ lemon

SERVES 4

HEAT 15G of the butter and the olive oil in a frying pan, then add the onion and garlic. Cook for 2–3 minutes until the onion is soft and golden.

DICE THE PANCETTA into small cubes. Add these to the pan and cook for 5 minutes on a low heat. Increase to a medium heat, and then add the lentils, along with a splash of white wine.

BRING THE CHICKEN STOCK to the boil in a separate pan. Add the chicken stock to the lentils one ladleful at a time, just as if making a risotto. Once the lentils are cooked and almost no stock remains, add the rest of the butter and mix well. Season with salt and pepper.

PUT THE POACHING LIQUID ingredients into a separate pan with 300ml of water and bring to the boil. Once the liquid is boiling, take the pan off the heat, add the cod and place a lid on the pan. After 5 minutes, turn the fish over, replace the lid and continue to cook off the heat for another 5 minutes.

ADD THE SPINACH, SPRING ONIONS and chopped parsley to the lentils and mix everything together well. Check the seasoning.

ADD THE POACHED COD TO THE LENTIL STEW and gently warm it through, basting the fish with the lentils.

JANSSON'S TEMPTATION

This is a wonderful Swedish dish and one that my Uncle Yonus
always serves when he does a smorgasbord.

1 tbsp olive oil
1 large onion, chopped
1 x 50g can of anchovies
    in oil
500g waxy potatoes, peeled
4–6 tbsp double cream
salt and freshly ground
    black pepper

SERVES 4

HEAT THE OLIVE OIL in a large frying pan. Add the onion and
anchovies and sauté until the onion is soft.

PREHEAT THE OVEN to 190°C/Fan 170°C/Gas mark 5.

CUT THE POTATOES into matchsticks and add them to the anchovy
mix. Check the seasoning and add salt if necessary and freshly
milled black pepper.

Tip the onions, anchovies and potatoes into an ovenproof dish
and add the cream. Bake for about 25 minutes until golden brown
and crispy on top.

POLLOCK WITH WHITE BEAN VINAIGRETTE

Cheaper than cod and just as tasty, pollock is becoming
more and more popular.

1 shallot, diced
120ml Chardonnay vinegar
4 piquillo peppers from a jar,
    drained and diced
1 x 400g can of haricot
    beans, drained
small handful of flatleaf
    parsley, chopped
2 tbsp Classic vinaigrette
    (see page 282)
2 baby gem lettuces
4 x 130g pollock fillets,
    skin on
2 tbsp olive oil
salt and freshly ground
    black pepper

SERVES 4

PUT THE DICED SHALLOT in a pan and pour in the Chardonnay
vinegar. Cook over a low heat until all the vinegar has evaporated
and the shallots are translucent. Add a pinch of salt.

MIX THE PIQUILLO PEPPERS with the haricot beans. Once the
shallots are ready, add them to the peppers and beans, then
mix well and add the chopped parsley. Mix in the vinaigrette
and check the seasoning.

SEPARATE THE LEAVES of the lettuces and cut them in half.

PREHEAT THE OVEN to 180°C/Fan 160°C/Gas mark 4. Season
the pollock on both sides. Heat the olive oil in a frying pan and
fry the fish until golden. Transfer the fish to a baking sheet
and cook in the preheated oven for 4–5 minutes.

ADD THE LETTUCE to the beans and peppers and serve with
the fish fillets on top.

POACHED POLLOCK WITH MUSTARD SAUCE AND POACHED EGG

25g butter
25g flour
500ml milk
2 tsp coarse grain mustard
1 tsp Dijon mustard
1 tbsp olive oil
4 x 100g pollock fillets,
   skin off
250g baby spinach
1 tbsp white wine vinegar
4 eggs
squeeze of lemon juice,
   for serving
salt and black pepper

SERVES 4

MELT THE BUTTER in a pan, stir in the flour and cook for 1 minute. Add the milk gradually, whisking it in until you have a smooth white sauce. Season with salt and pepper, then add both mustards and set the sauce aside in a warm place.

HEAT A TABLESPOON OF OIL in a frying pan and add the pollock. Cook for about 2 minutes on each side.

IN A SEPARATE PAN, wilt the spinach in the olive oil.

MEANWHILE, BRING A PAN OF WATER TO THE BOIL and add the white wine vinegar. Crack the eggs into separate bowls. Turn the heat down so the water is simmering gently and then give it a stir so it swirls in the pan. Add the eggs and cook for 3 minutes at a low simmer.

TO SERVE, place some wilted spinach on each plate, add a piece of pollock and glaze with mustard sauce. Add a a squeeze of lemon, then put a poached egg on top and serve immediately.

THAI FISH CAKES

This is a perfect little supper dish and a good way
of using up scraps of leftover fish.

500g white fish, such as
    cod, ling or pollock
1 tbsp Thai fish sauce
1 tbsp red curry paste
2 tbsp chopped coriander
2 spring onions, finely sliced
1 egg
pinch of dried chilli
juice and zest of 1 lime
2 tbsp plain flour, for
    dusting
sunflower or groundnut oil,
    for shallow frying
1 bunch of watercress

For the honey dip
2 tbsp honey
1 tbsp vinegar
1 small onion, finely
    chopped
2 tbsp tomato ketchup
1 tbsp chopped mint
    and coriander

SERVES 4

FIRST MAKE THE DIP. Put the honey in a small pan with the
vinegar, onion and ketchup. Bring to the boil, then remove
from the heat and leave to cool. Add the chopped herbs.

PUT ALL THE INGREDIENTS for the fish cakes, except the oil,
flour and watercress, in a food processor and blitz together.

SHAPE THE MIXTURE into small fish cakes and dust in flour.
Preheat the oven to 180°C/Fan 160°C/Gas mark 4.

HEAT THE OIL in a pan and shallow-fry the fish cakes until
golden brown. Transfer them to a baking sheet and put them
into the preheated oven for 5 minutes to heat through. Serve
with the honey dip and some watercress.

HALIBUT WITH ANCHOVIES AND CHIPS

l love the flavours of this dish. The saltiness of the anchovies
is just right with the chips and the tangy horseradish.

3 large Desiree potatoes
sunflower oil, for frying
   the chips
6 tbsp mayonnaise
1 tbsp horseradish relish
10 anchovies in brine,
   drained
30g Parmesan cheese,
   freshly grated
4 x 130g halibut fillets
2 tbsp olive oil
1 tbsp chopped fresh chervil
50g butter
125ml Chicken stock
   (see page 282)
1–2 tbsp chopped chives
salt and freshly ground
   black pepper

SERVES 4

PEEL THE POTATOES and cut them into chips. Heat a large frying pan half-filled with oil and fry the chips in batches until golden. Remove and drain on kitchen paper. Mix the mayonnaise with the horseradish, then roughly chop the anchovies. Set both aside.

PREHEAT THE OVEN to 180°C/Fan 160°C/Gas mark 4. Place the chips on a baking sheet, sprinkle with the Parmesan, then season with salt and pepper. Bake in the oven for 3–4 minutes, just long enough to melt the cheese but not burn the potatoes.

SEASON THE HALIBUT with salt. Heat 2 tablespoons of olive oil in a frying pan and colour the halibut on both sides, starting with the skin side. Once both sides are golden, sprinkle with chervil and add the butter and chicken stock.

COVER THE PAN with foil and cook the fish over a high heat for 2 minutes. Remove the foil, take the fish out of the pan and place on kitchen paper to drain. Reduce the remaining liquid in the pan until you have a sticky sauce. Use this sauce to baste the halibut.

TAKE THE CHIPS from the oven and sprinkle with the chopped anchovies and chopped chives. Serve with the halibut and horseradish mayonnaise.

OVEN-BAKED HALIBUT WITH CHORIZO AND BUTTER BEAN STEW

Fatty chorizo, white beans and halibut are a great combination.
Serve with a green salad.

2 ripe tomatoes
2 tbsp olive oil
1 garlic clove, finely chopped
100g Spanish chorizo,
　diced into 5mm cubes
1 red chilli, seeded and
　finely chopped
1 x 400g can of butter beans,
　drained
4 x 130g halibut fillets,
　skin removed
1 bunch of spring onions,
　chopped
2 baby gem lettuces
2 tbsp chopped flatleaf
　parsley
salt and freshly ground
　black pepper

CUT THE TOMATOES lengthwise into quarters, discard the seeds and cores, then dice the flesh. Heat 1 tablespoon of olive oil in a frying pan and sauté the garlic over a low heat for 1–2 minutes.

ADD THE DICED CHORIZO to the pan and cook for another 2–3 minutes, so the fat starts to run out of the chorizo.

ADD THE CHOPPED CHILLI, butter beans and diced tomato and continue to cook over a low heat for about 5 minutes. The oil of the chorizo should soon start to stain the beans red. Once everything is hot, taste the stew and season accordingly.

PREHEAT THE OVEN to 180°C/Fan 160°C/Gas mark 4 and line a baking sheet with baking parchment. Brush the halibut with the rest of the olive oil and season with salt and pepper. Place the fish on the baking sheet and bake in the oven for 7–10 minutes.

ADD THE SPRING ONIONS to the bean and chorizo stew. Separate the leaves of the baby gem lettuces and cut them into 4. Add the sliced lettuce leaves to the stew and continue to cook for another couple of minutes. Sprinkle with the chopped parsley.

SPOON THE STEW into large bowls, place the fish on top, and serve.

RED SNAPPER WITH SPICY COUSCOUS

If you feel you'd like more moisture in this dish, add a little vinegar
to the fish and double the amount of lemon on the couscous.

1 jar of piquillo peppers
(about 12)
150g couscous
2 tsp white wine vinegar
50ml olive oil, plus 2 tbsp
2 red chillies, seeded and
finely chopped
1 garlic clove, finely chopped
3 shallots, chopped
1 tbsp harissa
8 spring onions, chopped
small handful of chopped
chervil or basil
2–3 lemons
4 red snapper fillets, skin on
and pin-boned

SERVES 4

DRAIN THE OIL from the piquillo peppers and chop them roughly.
Mix the peppers with the raw couscous in a bowl.

POUR THE VINEGAR and 50ml of olive oil into a pan, add 150ml of
water and bring to the boil. Pour this liquid over the couscous and
peppers, then cover the bowl with cling film and leave it in a warm
place for 10 minutes. Take the cling film off the bowl and break up
the couscous with a fork.

HEAT 1 TABLESPOON of olive oil in a frying pan and add the
chopped chillies, garlic and shallots. Cook for 3–4 minutes over
a low heat, then add the harissa and cook for another 1–2 minutes.
Add this to the couscous and mix everything together well. Add
the chopped spring onions, chopped chervil or basil, then stir in
the zest of 1 lemon and the juice of half a lemon. Taste and add
more juice if required.

FRY THE SNAPPER FILLETS, skin-side down, in a tablespoon of oil
in a non-stick frying pan. When the skin is crispy, turn the fillets
over and finish cooking on the other side for 2 minutes. They
should take 3–4 minutes in all.

SERVE THE COUSCOUS onto the plates, place the fish on top and
add a squeeze of lemon to finish.

HADDOCK WITH PARSLEY AND MUSTARD

A quintessentially English recipe and excellent when prepared carefully. Make sure you use really good Dijon mustard.

40g flatleaf parsley, chopped
200g white breadcrumbs
4 x 130g haddock fillets, skinned
1 tbsp olive oil
4 tsp Dijon mustard
salt and freshly ground black pepper

SERVES 4

PUT THE PARSLEY in a food processor and blend to a paste. Add the breadcrumbs and blend until you get a sand-like powder.

PAT THE HADDOCK FILLETS with kitchen paper to remove any excess moisture. Season with salt and pepper.

PREHEAT THE OVEN to 180°C/Fan 160°C/Gas mark 4 and line a baking sheet with baking parchment. Heat the olive oil in a frying pan and gently colour the haddock on one side for about 2 minutes. Turn the fillets over and transfer them to the baking sheet.

PAINT EACH HADDOCK with a layer of mustard and then sprinkle with the parsley and breadcrumb mixture. Bake in the oven for 7 minutes or until the flesh breaks away without resistance.

MONKFISH WITH OLIVES AND PANCETTA

Be careful when seasoning this dish, as you have the natural saltiness of the olives and bacon.

2 tsp curry powder
2 tsp salt
2 tbsp olive oil
4 x 150g portions of
  monkfish, off the bone
  and skin removed
120g pancetta
2 baby gem lettuces
120g pitted black olives,
  cut in half
250g cherry tomatoes,
  cut in half
small handful of fresh
  basil leaves, chopped
balsamic vinegar, for
  drizzling
salt and freshly ground
  black pepper

SERVES 4

PREHEAT THE OVEN to 180°C/Fan 160°C/Gas mark 4. Mix the curry powder with the salt and season the fish with this mixture.

HEAT THE OLIVE OIL in a frying pan and cook the monkfish on a high heat for about 2 minutes, until golden on all sides. Transfer the fish to a baking sheet and bake in the oven for 6–8 minutes or until cooked through. Halfway through the cooking time, turn the fish over so it cooks evenly on both sides.

WHILE THE FISH IS COOKING, cut the pancetta into thin strips and fry until golden, adding a touch of oil if you need.

SEPARATE THE LEAVES of the lettuces and shred them with a sharp knife. Add the shredded lettuce and the olives to the pancetta and cook on a high heat. Once the lettuce has started to cook down, add the cherry tomatoes to the pan. Season to taste.

ADD SOME CHOPPED BASIL and spoon the mixture onto serving plates. Place the monkfish on top and drizzle a few drops of balsamic vinegar around the plate.

DOVER SOLE WITH BUTTER AND BROWN SHRIMP

Dover sole is an expensive fish but lovely to cook at home for a real treat. Cheaper alternatives would be plaice or slip soles.

4 Dover soles, both skins removed (ask the fishmonger to do this for you)
plain flour, for dusting
2 tbsp olive oil
80g butter
80g capers
150g peeled brown shrimp
2 tbsp chopped flatleaf parsley
squeeze of lemon juice, for serving
salt and freshly ground black pepper

SERVES 4

TAKE EACH SOLE and hold it firmly, one hand at the head and the other at the tail, then pull as hard as you can. This straightens the spine so that the sole will not curl up when cooking. The fish can be slippery, so hold it with kitchen paper. Season the soles on both sides with salt, then dust with flour.

HEAT THE OLIVE OIL in a large frying pan and cook the fish for 2–3 minutes on each side. Once the fish is golden, add the butter and continue to cook. When the butter begins to foam, use a spoon to baste the foam over the fish.

CHECK THAT THE SOLES ARE COOKED by pressing the back of a thin fork into the flesh, which should be soft and offer no resistance. Remove the fish from the pan and place on the serving plate.

ADD THE CAPERS AND SHRIMP to the pan with the foaming butter and sauté for 2–3 minutes. Add the chopped parsley, season to taste and finish with a squeeze of lemon juice.

SPOON THE SHRIMP and capers over the soles to serve.

SEA BREAM WITH LEEKS, CHORIZO AND POTATOES

The little fricassee of vegetables and chorizo is just right with the fish and you can adapt it according to what you have available. If you don't have leeks, for example, use peppers or more tomatoes.

4 x 150g sea bream fillets, skin on, scaled and pin-boned
5–6 tbsp olive oil
150g small new potatoes, cut in half
100g chorizo sausage, diced into 1cm cubes
1 leek, thinly sliced
250g cherry tomatoes, cut in half
a few fresh thyme sprigs, chopped
small handful of flatleaf parsley, chopped
squeeze of lemon juice, for serving
salt and freshly ground black pepper

SERVES 4

CHECK THAT ALL THE PIN BONES have been removed from the fish and pull out any that remain with a pair of tweezers. Take a sharp knife and score the fillets at 1cm intervals on the skin side. Season with salt and pepper.

HEAT 1–2 TABLESPOONS OF OLIVE OIL in a heavy-based frying pan and fry the potatoes for about 8 minutes, until cooked and golden.

ADD THE DICED CHORIZO to the pan and cook for another 2–3 minutes. The oil of the chorizo should start to stain the potatoes red. Add the leek and continue to cook over a high heat for 2–3 minutes, but don't allow the leek slices to brown. Add the cherry tomatoes, stir in the chopped herbs and season to taste.

HEAT THE REST OF OLIVE OIL in a separate pan. Add the bream fillets, skin-side down, and pan-fry for 3 minutes until golden. Turn the fish over and continue to cook for another minute until the flesh breaks away without resistance.

SPOON THE POTATO, chorizo and tomato mixture onto serving plates and place the bream fillets on top. Finish with a squeeze of lemon juice.

CAKES
AND
PUDDINGS

LIZ'S BANANA BREAD

My good friend Liz is a brilliant chef and this cake is one of her signature recipes. She always makes it for parties and it's absolutely delicious.

100g sultanas
75ml rum
4 small, ripe bananas
125g plain flour
2 tsp baking powder
½ tsp bicarbonate of soda
½ tsp salt
25g butter, plus extra for greasing the tin
150g caster sugar
2 large eggs
60g walnuts, roughly chopped

MAKES 1 LOAF (12 SLICES)

PUT THE SULTANAS in a bowl with the rum and leave to soak.

GREASE A 900G LOAF TIN with butter and line it with greaseproof paper. Preheat the oven to 170°C/Fan 150°C/Gas 3½.

PEEL AND MASH THE BANANAS – you need about 300g in all.

SIFT THE FLOUR with the baking powder, bicarbonate of soda and salt.

MELT THE BUTTER, then mix it with the sugar in a large bowl. Beat in the eggs, then add the flour mixture and stir well. Add the mashed bananas, walnuts, sultanas and rum.

SPOON THE MIXTURE into the prepared tin and bake for 45–60 minutes or until a skewer inserted into the centre comes out clean. Leave to cool in the tin, before turning out. Store in an airtight cake tin.

COFFEE AND WALNUT CAKE

Baking is back in fashion and it is nice to have a cake in the kitchen to offer to visitors. This is one my mum used to make when I was younger and it's an all-time classic.

110g caster sugar
110g butter
2 eggs, beaten
110g self-raising flour, sifted
1 tbsp espresso coffee

For the topping
250g mascarpone
75g sugar
2 tsp espresso coffee
75g walnuts, chopped

MAKES 1 X 23CM CAKE

PREHEAT THE OVEN to 180°C/Fan 160°C/Gas mark 4. Grease and line a 23cm cake tin.

PUT THE SUGAR AND BUTTER in a bowl and beat well until light and fluffy. Add the beaten eggs, a little at a time, beating well after each addition. Gradually fold in the sifted flour, then add the coffee.

GENTLY SPOON THE MIXTURE into the tin and cook in the preheated oven for 25 minutes. To check that the cake is done, insert a skewer into the middle – it should come out clean. If not, cook the cake for another 5 minutes. Leave to cool in the tin for 10 minutes, then turn out onto a wire rack to cool completely.

TO MAKE THE TOPPING, whip the mascarpone with the sugar and coffee.

WHEN THE CAKE IS COOL, split it in half through the middle to make 2 layers. Spread some of the mascarpone mixture on one half, then put the other layer on top and add the rest of the mascarpone over the top of the cake. Decorate with the chopped walnuts.

CHOCOLATE BROWNIES

Don't be afraid to take these out of the oven while they're still squidgy in the middle. They will carry on cooking for a while and you don't want them to be dry. Use good chocolate –at least 70 percent cocoa solids.

3 eggs
210g caster sugar
125g bitter chocolate
200g butter, plus extra
    for greasing the tin
100g flour, plus extra
    for dusting the tin
125g walnuts, roughly
    chopped

MAKES 12 SQUARES

PREHEAT THE OVEN to 160°C/Fan 140°C/Gas mark 3. Using an electric whisk, beat the eggs and caster sugar together until pale and creamy.

BREAK UP THE CHOCOLATE and place it with the butter in a bowl over a pan of simmering water until both are melted. Take care the bottom of the bowl does not touch the water. Leave to cool slightly, then add the chocolate mix to the eggs and sugar. Fold together using a spatula, then add the flour and chopped walnuts and fold again carefully.

YOU NEED A 15 x 25cm or a 20 x 20cm baking tin. Grease the tin with butter, then line it with greased greaseproof paper and sprinkle with flour. Pour the brownie mixture into the baking tin and bake in the preheated oven for 25 minutes – the centre should be slightly gooey. Leave to cool in the tin, then cut into squares.

STICKY LEMON DRIZZLE AND POPPY SEED CAKE

I like this sort of cake and it tastes even better the day after it is made. Don't be afraid of the sticky topping – it works well. You could also try making an orange version.

175g unsalted butter, plus
    extra for greasing the tin
175g caster sugar
3 eggs, beaten
175g self-raising flour
finely grated zest of
    2 lemons
25g poppy seeds

For sticky lemon topping
4 tbsp caster sugar
6 tbsp fondant icing sugar
about 4 tbsp lemon juice

MAKES 1 LOAF

PREHEAT THE OVEN to 180°C/Fan 160°C/Gas mark 4. Grease a 900g loaf tin and line it with baking parchment. You need to allow enough parchment to extend above the sides of the tin – this makes it easier to lift the cake out.

CREAM THE BUTTER AND CASTER SUGAR together until pale, light and fluffy, then beat in the eggs one at a time.

FOLD THE FLOUR INTO THE MIXTURE, and then stir in the lemon zest, poppy seeds and 4 tablespoons of water.

POUR THE MIXTURE into the prepared tin and bake for about 30–40 minutes.

TO MAKE THE STICKY TOPPING, put the caster sugar in a pan with 3 tablespoons of water and heat until the sugar dissolves. Boil for 2 minutes.

WHEN THE CAKE IS COOKED, prick the top with a skewer and pour over the sticky sugar topping. Leave the cake to cool in the tin, then carefully lift it out using the lining paper.

MIX THE FONDANT ICING SUGAR with the lemon juice and spoon this over the cake.

GINGERBREAD

Good gingerbread is one of the best of all cakes and one my mum has always made. Like all cakes, this needs to be made carefully, with ingredients properly measured and added in the correct order. Not something to be slapdash about.

225g plain flour
½ tsp salt
1 tsp bicarbonate of soda
3 tsp ground ginger
1 tsp ground cinnamon
75g butter
100g soft brown sugar
100g black treacle
   (about 2 tbsp)
100g golden syrup
   (about 2 tbsp)
2 eggs
6 tbsp milk
50g sultanas
50g preserved ginger,
   chopped
25g candied peel, chopped
50g blanched flaked
   almonds

**MAKES 1 X 20CM
SQUARE CAKE**

PREHEAT THE OVEN to 160°C/Fan 140°C/Gas mark 3. Grease a 20cm square cake tin and line it with baking parchment.

SIFT THE FLOUR, salt, bicarbonate of soda, ginger and cinnamon into a bowl and set aside.

PLACE THE BUTTER into a saucepan and add the sugar, treacle and syrup. Warm gently over a low heat until the butter has just melted and the ingredients are blended. Remove from the heat and set aside until it has cooled to about body temperature.

LIGHTLY MIX THE EGGS and milk and stir them into the butter mixture. Mix thoroughly. Then pour this into the centre of the flour in the bowl and mix with a wooden spoon until smooth and glossy. Stir in the sultanas, ginger and candied peel.

POUR THE MIXTURE into the lined cake tin and sprinkle with flaked almonds. Bake in the centre of the preheated oven for about 1 hour. Do not open the oven for the first 40 minutes or the cake may sink in the middle.

WHEN THE CAKE IS DONE, remove it from the oven, turn it onto a wire rack and leave to cool.

AMARETTO CAKE

This is a recipe from my cousin Antonia, who is a very good cook. It does work best made in a cake tin with a hole in the middle, as the mixture is very dense. If the cake starts to get too brown during the cooking, cover the top with a piece of foil.

200g amaretti biscuits
1 glass of Amaretto or sherry
250g plain flour, plus a little
    extra for the tin
2 tsp baking powder
220g butter or margarine,
    room temperature, plus
    extra for greasing the tin
220g caster sugar, plus extra
    for sprinkling on cake
pinch of salt
4 eggs
50g chopped almonds
50g ground almonds
grated zest of 1 lemon
2 tsp vanilla extract
milk or yoghurt, if necessary

MAKES 1 X 20CM CAKE

PREHEAT THE OVEN to 160°C/Fan 140°C/Gas mark 3. Grease a 23cm cake tin and sprinkle the inside with flour.

CRUSH THE AMARETTI BISCUITS IN A BOWL and add the Amaretto or sherry. Sift the flour and baking powder into a separate bowl.

BEAT THE BUTTER AND SUGAR with the salt in another bowl. Add the eggs, one at a time, with a spoonful of the flour mixture each time, and beat well. Add the chopped and ground almonds, then the rest of the flour, the lemon zest and vanilla extract.

IF THE MIXTURE IS TOO THICK, add a little milk or yoghurt until it is a dropping consistency.

POUR HALF THE MIXTURE INTO THE PREPARED TIN, even it out with a spatula or palette knife, then place the crushed amaretti biscuits on top. Cover with the rest of the mixture and sprinkle the top with sugar. Place in the preheated oven for 1 hour.

REMOVE THE CAKE from the oven and leave to cool in the tin for 5 minutes. Turn out onto a wire rack and leave to cool completely. Serve on its own or with cream.

SCOTTI'S LA CAPRESE CHOCOLATE CAKE

One of my best friends is from the Italian island of Ischia and this wonderful cake is one of his favourite recipes. He's a great cook, but he doesn't get to the stove often enough for my liking!

200g unsalted butter, at
   room temperature, plus
   extra for greasing the tin
200g caster sugar
4 eggs, separated
200g dark chocolate,
   broken into pieces
200g ground almonds

MAKES 1 X 23CM CAKE

PREHEAT THE OVEN to 160°C/Fan 140°C/Gas mark 3. Grease a 23cm cake tin and line it with baking parchment.

BEAT THE BUTTER AND SUGAR with an electric whisk until light and creamy. Add the egg yolks, beating them in well.

MELT THE CHOCOLATE in a bowl over a pan of simmering water, then add it to the mixture.

BEAT THE EGG WHITES until they form stiff peaks and then gently fold them into the chocolate mix. Add the ground almonds, being careful not to overwork the mixture.

SPOON THE MIXTURE into the lined cake tin and bake in the middle of the preheated oven for 40–45 minutes. Test with a skewer, which should come out dry. If not, put the cake back into the oven for another 5 minutes.

WHEN THE CAKE IS DONE, remove it from the oven and turn it out onto a wire rack to cool.

VANILLA CHEESECAKE WITH BLUEBERRIES

This is an easy cheesecake to make and it sets quickly. The lemon adds a welcome freshness, or you can use orange juice if you want a change. Use any seasonal berries.

150g digestive biscuits
100g butter, melted,
    plus extra for greasing
350g cream cheese
70g icing sugar
2 tsp lemon juice
grated zest of 1 lemon
½ tsp vanilla extract
300ml double cream
200g blueberries
2 tbsp caster sugar

SERVES 8

GREASE A 20CM loose-bottomed cake tin. Put the digestive biscuits into a plastic bag and crush them with a rolling pin. Mix them with the melted butter, then press the mixture into the tin in an even layer.

MIX THE CREAM CHEESE in a bowl with the icing sugar, lemon juice and zest, and the vanilla. In a separate bowl, whisk the cream and then fold it into the cream cheese mix.

SPOON THE FILLING onto the biscuit base and smooth the top with a spatula. Place in the fridge for a couple of hours to set.

MEANWHILE, PUT THE BLUEBERRIES in a pan with the caster sugar and cook them gently. Leave to cool.

WHEN THE CHEESECAKE IS READY, remove it from the tin, spoon the blueberries over the top and serve.

LEMON AND RASPBERRY TART

You'd think that raspberries and lemon would be too sharp, but they work very well together. If you don't feel like making the lemon filling, you can use a good lemon curd – easy to find at farmers' markets these days. Just spoon it over the cooked pastry base and add the raspberries on top – no need to cook.

4 medium eggs
200g sugar
125g whipping cream
130ml lemon juice, plus
    grated zest of the lemons
200g raspberries
icing sugar, for dusting

For the sweet pastry
330g plain flour, plus
    extra for rolling out
pinch of salt
100g icing sugar
200g cold butter, diced
3 eggs

SERVES 6

FIRST, MAKE THE SWEET PASTRY. Sift the flour, salt and sugar into a bowl. Add the butter and rub it in with your fingertips until the mixture resembles breadcrumbs – you can do this in a food processor if you prefer. Beat 2 of the eggs, add them to the bowl and mix well to form a dough, but don't overwork. Wrap the dough in cling film and leave it to rest in the fridge for at least an hour before using.

PREHEAT THE OVEN to 180°C/Fan 160°C/Gas mark 4. Roll out the pastry on a floured surface until it is only about 2mm thick – be careful not to break it! Use the pastry to line a 24cm loose-bottomed, fluted tart tin. Cover the pastry with a piece of baking parchment and fill it with baking beans, rice or dried pasta. Bake in the oven for 20 minutes or until the crust starts to turn golden.

ONCE THE TART SHELL IS COOKED, remove it from the oven and discard the baking beans. Beat the remaining egg and use it to paint the inside of the pastry case. Put the pastry back in the oven for just 2 minutes so that the egg cooks, then take it out, paint with more egg and bake for another 2 minutes – this will fix any holes in the pastry and seal the base. Turn the oven down to 110°C/Fan 90°C/Gas mark ¼.

NOW MAKE THE LEMON FILLING. Whisk the eggs with the sugar until all the sugar has dissolved. Add the cream, lemon juice and the grated zest. Pour the lemon mixture into the pastry case and bake in the oven for 45 minutes until the filling is set. Leave to cool.

ONCE THE TART IS COOL, carefully place the raspberries on top. Dust with icing sugar to serve.

FIG AND WALNUT CROSTATA

Figs and walnuts are a perfect marriage, but make sure
the figs are nice and ripe – this is a recipe to make when
they are in season. It tastes even better the next day.

1 quantity of sweet pastry
   (see page 246)
4 eggs, beaten
60g black treacle
90g golden syrup
½ tsp vanilla extract
125g figs, diced
100g walnuts, chopped

SERVES 8

PREHEAT THE OVEN to 180°C/Fan 160°C/Gas mark 4.

ROLL OUT THE PASTRY to a thickness of 3mm and use it to line
a 30cm flan tin. Line the pastry case with baking parchment and
fill it with baking beans, rice or dried pasta. Bake in the oven for
15 minutes. Remove the beans and paper and return the pastry
case to the oven for another 5 minutes. Remove and set aside to
cool. Leave the oven on.

MIX THE EGGS with the treacle, syrup and vanilla in a bowl. Put
the figs and walnuts in a separate bowl and mix them together.

SPREAD THE FIGS AND WALNUTS over the bottom of the pastry
case, then pour on the egg and treacle mix. Bake in the preheated
oven for 20 minutes until just cooked. Leave to cool in the tart tin
before serving.

PRUNE TART

I love this dessert, which we used to serve in Murano when we
first opened. Serve with vanilla ice cream or fromage blanc.

175g prunes
50ml Armagnac
1 quantity of sweet pastry
   (see page 246)
125g butter, at room
   temperature
125g caster sugar
3 eggs, beaten
125g ground almonds
1 tsp cornflour

SERVES 8

MARINATE THE PRUNES in the Armagnac for 30 minutes.
Preheat the oven to 190°C/Fan 170°C/Gas mark 5.

ROLL OUT THE PASTRY to a thickness of 3mm and use it to line
a 28cm loose-bottomed flan tin. Trim the edges neatly, prick the
base and leave to rest for 15 minutes in the fridge.

TO MAKE THE ALMOND CREAM, whisk the butter and sugar until
light and fluffy. Add the eggs, a little at a time, then mix in the
almonds and cornflour.

SPREAD THE ALMOND CREAM over the pastry case. Add the
marinated prunes on top and cook for 30 minutes until the tart is
golden brown. Leave to cool, then remove from the tin and serve.

CHOCOLATE PECAN TART

This is good for a dinner party, as it looks more complicated than it is and it can be prepared in advance. If you want to be really fancy, add some shavings of white or dark chocolate on top.

1 quantity of sweet pastry
(see page 246)
1 egg

For the filling
400g dark chocolate,
broken into pieces
250ml whipping cream
150ml milk
2 eggs, beaten
100g pecan nuts, chopped

SERVES 6-8

PREHEAT THE OVEN to 180°C/Fan 160°C/Gas mark 4. Roll out the pastry to a thickness of 3mm and use it to line a 20cm flan tin. Line the pastry case with baking parchment and fill it with baking beans, rice or dried pasta. Bake in the oven for 15 minutes.

ONCE THE TART SHELL IS COOKED, remove it from the oven and discard the baking beans. Beat the egg and use it to paint the inside of the pastry case. Put the pastry back in the oven for 2 minutes so that the egg cooks, then take it out, paint with more egg and bake for another 2 minutes – this will fix any holes in the pastry and seal the base. Leave the oven on.

PUT THE CHOCOLATE in a bowl over a pan of gently simmering water until it melts. Make sure the bottom of the bowl doesn't touch the water.

HEAT THE CREAM AND MILK to boiling point in a separate pan. Add this to the melted chocolate and mix until smooth. Leave to cool slightly until just warm, rather than hot.

ADD THE EGGS and beat until smooth. Pour the mixture into the pastry case and scatter with the pecan nuts. Bake in the preheated oven for 20 minutes. Cool, then leave to set in the fridge. Serve at room temperature.

APPLE AND BLACKBERRY PIE

This is one of those combinations that just works and it's one of my mum's favourites. She's very generous with her pies but not with her pie dishes, which she always wants back. She even marks them with nail varnish so we can't steal them.

3–4 Bramley apples
4 tbsp caster sugar,
   plus extra for sprinkling
   on top of the pie
1 tsp cinnamon
200g blackberries
1 tbsp milk

For the shortcrust pastry
250g flour
1 tsp sugar
pinch of salt
150g cold butter
1 tbsp milk
1 egg

SERVES 6

MAKE THE SHORTCRUST PASTRY. Mix the flour, sugar and salt in a bowl. Add the butter and rub it in with your fingertips until the mixture resembles breadcrumbs. Mix the milk with the egg and start to fold this into the flour mixture, adding just enough to make a smooth dough. Wrap the pastry in cling film and leave it to rest in the fridge for 20 minutes.

PREHEAT THE OVEN to 180°C/Fan 160°C/Gas mark 4. Roll out half the pastry on a floured surface to an area about 2cm wider than your pie dish.

PEEL AND CORE THE APPLES and slice them into the dish. Add the sugar, cinnamon and blackberries.

ROLL OUT the rest of the pastry and place it on top of the pie. Trim off any excess pastry and crimp the edges together to seal. Cut a couple of slashes in the top, then paint the pastry with milk. Bake in the preheated oven for 30–35 minutes, or until golden. Serve with cream or ice cream.

GINGER STEAMED PUDDING

If you should chance to have any of this pudding left over, don't worry as it is even better the next day. Just resteam for a while to warm it up.

180g softened butter,
  plus extra for greasing
  the basin
6 tbsp golden syrup
180g plain flour
3 tsp baking powder
180g caster sugar
60g stem ginger from a jar,
  chopped finely, plus
  3 tbsp of the ginger syrup
3 eggs

SERVES 6

GREASE a 1-litre pudding basin with a little butter and add 4 tablespoons of the syrup.

PUT THE REMAINING INGREDIENTS, including the 180g of butter and the rest of the golden syrup into a bowl. Using an electric whisk, mix everything together until smooth.

POUR THE MIXTURE into the basin and cover with a piece of greaseproof paper. Take a piece of foil and make a pleat down the middle, then place this over the pudding basin and tie it in place.

PLACE AN UPTURNED SAUCER or a ramekin in a large deep saucepan and sit the pudding on top. Fill the pan with boiling water to about half-way up the basin. Place a lid on the pan and steam for 2 hours on top of the stove. Top up with boiling water as necessary. Remove the foil and greaseproof and insert a skewer into the centre of the pudding – if it comes out clean, the pudding is done. If not, cook the pudding for another 15 minutes – be sure to check there is enough water in the pan.

CAREFULLY REMOVE the pudding from the pan. Loosen the edges by running a knife around the pudding and turn out onto a plate. Serve with custard or cream.

TREACLE PUDDING

Everyone loves a treacle pud. When we first put this on the menu at York and Albany it sold like the clappers and regulars demanded it. You can vary this basic recipe as you like – for example, use marmalade instead of syrup.

3 tbsp golden syrup
180g plain flour
3 tsp baking powder
180g softened butter,
  plus extra for greasing
  the basin
3 eggs
180g demerara sugar
1 tbsp black treacle

SERVES 6

GREASE a 1-litre pudding basin with butter and add the golden syrup. Using an electric whisk, mix the flour, baking powder, butter, eggs, sugar and treacle in a separate bowl until well combined.

POUR THE MIXTURE into the basin and cover with a piece of greaseproof paper. Take a piece of foil and make a pleat down the middle, then place this over the pudding basin and tie it in place.

PLACE AN UPTURNED SAUCER or a ramekin in a large deep saucepan and sit the pudding on top. Fill the pan with boiling water to about half way up the basin. Place a lid on the pan and steam for 2 hours and 15 minutes on top of the stove. Top up with boiling water as necessary. Towards the end of the cooking time you will see that the pudding has risen up – a sign that it is ready. If you want to check, remove the foil and greaseproof and insert a skewer into the centre of the pudding – if it comes out clean, the pudding is done. If not, cook the pudding for another 15 minutes – be sure to check there is enough water in the pan.

CAREFULLY REMOVE the pudding from the pan. Loosen the edges by running a knife around the pudding and turn out onto a plate.

BAKED APPLES

This is one of those perfect puddings – you just put it in the oven and it takes care of itself. It's also a good way of using up nuts and dried fruit.

4 Braeburn apples
large knob of soft butter
30g sugar
crème fraîche, for serving

For the filling
50g ground almonds
25g flaked almonds
4 tbsp raisins
1 tbsp muscovado sugar
1 tsp cinnamon
2 tbsp honey
a splash of Calvados

SERVES 4

PREHEAT THE OVEN to 180°C/Fan 160°C/Gas mark 4. Remove the centres of the apples with a corer. You need to make a large enough hole for the filling, but be careful not to pierce all the way through to the bottom. Spread the apples with soft butter and then roll them in the sugar so that they are well coated. Set them aside.

TO MAKE THE FILLING, simply mix all the ingredients in a bowl until well combined. Stuff the apples with the filling and place them in an ovenproof dish – it should be just big enough to hold the apples tightly. Add a couple of tablespoons of water to the dish.

BAKE THE APPLES in the preheated oven for 30–40 minutes, or until they are soft and golden and the filling is bubbling. Serve the apples with a spoonful of crème fraîche.

HONEY-BAKED ORANGES WITH ROSEMARY

You only need the seeds from the vanilla pod in this recipe,
but don't throw out the pod. Put it in your caster sugar jar and you'll
have wonderful vanilla-flavoured sugar to use in desserts.

4 juicing oranges (ideally
   with very thin skin
   and loads of pulp)
3 tbsp Acacia honey
30g butter, diced
4 tbsp Cointreau
2–3 rosemary sprigs
4 tbsp muscovado sugar
½ vanilla pod
200ml double cream
50g caster sugar

SERVES 4

PREHEAT THE OVEN to 180°C/Fan 160°C/Gas mark 4. Wash the oranges and cut each one into quarters and discard any seeds. Place them in a high-sided baking tin that is just large enough to accommodate them all and drizzle with honey. Add the diced butter, Cointreau, rosemary and muscovado sugar and bake in the preheated oven for 25–30 minutes, or until the oranges are just starting to darken.

REMOVE THE ORANGE QUARTERS from the baking tin and strain the cooking juices into a pan. Bring the juices to the boil and cook for 6–8 minutes until they start to thicken. Place the oranges in serving bowls and pour the sauce over them.

SPLIT OPEN THE VANILLA POD and scrape out the seeds. Mix the seeds with the cream, then whisk until the cream thickens and forms soft peaks. Add the sugar and continue to whisk until stiff. Serve the oranges with a generous dollop of the vanilla cream.

PAVLOVA

This is a slightly different version of one of my favourite desserts. It might look like a lot of work but it's actually very simple to do – and impressive. Make this in late April and May, when the best Alphonso mangoes from India are in the shops.

4 egg whites
pinch of salt
225g caster sugar, plus
    2 tbsp
450ml whipping cream
2 drops of vanilla extract
2 large ripe mangoes,
    peeled and sliced
icing sugar, sifted

SERVES 4-6

PREHEAT THE OVEN to 160°C/Fan 140°C/Gas mark 3.

PUT THE EGG WHITES in a large mixing bowl with a pinch of salt and whip to soft peaks. Gradually add the 225g of caster sugar and continue whisking until the mixture forms stiff peaks.

DRAW A CIRCLE of about 20–23cm on a piece of greaseproof paper. Place a few dots of the meringue on a baking sheet and place the greaseproof on the sheet – the meringue dots will keep it in place. Spoon the meringue onto the circle, leaving a shallower layer in the centre.

PUT THE MERINGUE into the preheated oven and immediately reduce the heat to 110°C/Fan 90°C/Gas mark ¼. Bake for 1½ hours, then remove it from the oven and leave to cool.

WHIP THE CREAM to soft peaks and add a touch of vanilla and 2 tablespoons of caster sugar. Spoon the cream into the centre of the cooled meringue, then add the mango slices and finish with some sifted icing sugar.

FRIED FIGS WITH HONEY

This always makes me feel like I'm on holiday and it's particularly good in September when figs are at their best. Fabulous served with vanilla ice cream.

12 ripe figs, cut in half
knob of butter
1 tbsp acacia honey

SERVES 4

WASH THE FIGS and cut them in half, then pat them dry with kitchen paper.

HEAT THE BUTTER IN A PAN until it turns golden brown. Add the figs and sauté them gently, then add the honey and stir until it melts. Remove from the heat.

SERVE THE FIGS with the buttery honey juices poured over them and some vanilla ice cream.

VANILLA ICE CREAM

250ml double cream
250ml milk
½ vanilla pod
5 egg yolks
50g sugar

SERVES 4

POUR THE CREAM AND MILK into a pan and add the seeds scraped from the vanilla pod. Bring to the boil.

WHIP UP THE EGG YOLKS and sugar in a bowl, then add a touch of the hot milk mixture and stir immediately. Pour this into the pan with the milk and cream and cook slowly, stirring constantly until it coats the back of a spoon.

REMOVE THE PAN FROM THE HEAT and place it over a bowl of ice to cool the mixture. Churn in an ice-cream machine for 25–30 minutes until set. Transfer the ice cream to a container and freeze until ready to serve.

ALMOND PANNACOTTA

The addition of almonds gives a twist to the classic pannacotta. You can use metal dariole moulds or china ramekins for these and leave the puddings in the moulds instead of turning them out if you're nervous.

150g flaked almonds
500ml milk
500ml double cream
150g caster sugar
6 gelatine leaves

For the garnish
150g blackberries
4 tbsp icing sugar
75g flaked almonds

SERVES 6

PREHEAT THE OVEN to 180°C/Fan 160°C/Gas mark 4. Spread the almonds out on a baking sheet and toast them in the oven for 5–6 minutes until golden brown.

WHILE THE ALMONDS are toasting, pour the milk into a pan and add the cream and sugar. Bring to the boil, then remove the pan from the heat. Once the almonds are browned, add them to the pan with the milk. Cover the pan with a lid or cling film and set the mixture aside for 10 minutes off the heat.

PUT THE GELATINE LEAVES in a bowl and cover with cold water and ice cubes. Bring the milk mixture back to the boil. Squeeze out the gelatine leaves and add them to the hot milk, then remove from the heat. Pour the mixture into a blender and process for 1 minute at a low speed. Pass the mixture through a fine sieve and then pour into 6 x 130ml dariole moulds. Leave to set in the fridge for 3–4 hours.

TO PREPARE THE GARNISH, mix the blackberries with the icing sugar. Toast the almonds in the oven as above. Once the pannacottas are set, dip the base of each one very quickly into hot water to loosen, then turn onto individual plates. Add a few spoonfuls of the blackberries and some of the juice. Sprinkle over the toasted almonds and serve.

BAKED CHOCOLATE PUDDINGS

These little puds are incredibly delicious, but do be careful
not to overcook them – the centres must be gooey.

225g dark chocolate,
  70% cocoa solids
225g butter, cut into cubes
100g plain flour
300g caster sugar
4 egg yolks
5 whole eggs
cocoa powder

SERVES 6

PREHEAT THE OVEN to 180°C/160°Fan/Gas 4.

BREAK UP THE DARK CHOCOLATE and put it in a bowl with
the butter. Place the bowl over a pan of simmering water until
the chocolate and butter have melted. Take care the bottom
of the bowl does not touch the water. Allow to cool slightly.

SIFT THE FLOUR with the caster sugar into a bowl. Mix the egg
yolks with the whole eggs in a separate bowl. Stir the eggs into
the flour and sugar, then add the mixture to the melted chocolate
and butter, stirring everything together gently.

BUTTER 6 X 130ML DARIOLE MOULDS and sprinkle the insides
with cocoa powder, then spoon in the chocolate mixture. Bake in
the preheated oven for 10 minutes – the puddings should still be
soft to the touch as the centres must be slightly runny. Leave to
rest for 2 minutes before turning the puddings out of the moulds.

GINGER
CRÈME BRÛLÉE

I like ginger in desserts and I think it works brilliantly in this variation on the classic French burnt cream. Make sure you allow enough time for the mixture to infuse, and taste it after 10 minutes to make sure it is gingery enough.

500ml double cream
1 vanilla pod
50g fresh root ginger, sliced
100g caster sugar
8 large egg yolks
250ml milk
100g demerara sugar,
    for the brûlée top

**MAKES ENOUGH FOR
4 X 200ML RAMEKINS**

POUR THE CREAM into a saucepan. Split the vanilla pod in half and scrape out the seeds. Add the seeds, pod, ginger and half the sugar to the cream and bring it to the boil. Take it off the heat, cover the pan with a lid and leave for at least 10 minutes so that all the flavours can infuse into the cream.

PREHEAT THE OVEN to 160°C/Fan 140°C/Gas mark 3. Beat the egg yolks in a bowl with the remaining sugar until light and pale. Slowly pour the cream mix through a sieve onto the egg yolks, then immediately whisk in the cold milk to prevent the egg yolks from cooking. Pour into individual ramekins.

PLACE THE RAMEKINS IN A BAKING DISH. Add warm water to come halfway up the sides of the ramekins and steam in the preheated oven for 35 minutes. When done, they should be just set but still wobble a bit in the centre.

LEAVE TO COOL, ideally overnight.

TO SERVE, sprinkle with the demerara sugar, then caramelise with a chef's blowtorch. If you don't have a blowtorch, put the brûlées under a hot grill to caramelise.

HOT CHOCOLATE FUDGE SUNDAES

225g plain chocolate,
  broken into pieces
1 x 170g can of evaporated
  milk
2 tbsp rum
25g butter
75g mixed nuts (almonds,
  Brazil nuts, hazelnuts
  or pistachios)
2 tbsp honey
1 x 500ml tub of vanilla ice
  cream (or see page 266)

SERVES 4

MELT THE CHOCOLATE in a bowl set over a pan of gently simmering water. Do not allow the bottom of the bowl to touch the water.

TAKE THE BOWL OFF THE HEAT and add the evaporated milk and rum to the melted chocolate. Mix well and set aside.

MELT THE BUTTER in a frying pan, add the nuts and toast them lightly. Add the honey and stir until the nuts are caramelised, then remove from the heat and leave to cool. Chop the nuts once cool.

WHEN YOU ARE READY TO SERVE, pour the sauce into a pan and warm it through gently over a very low heat.

PUT SCOOPS OF VANILLA ICE CREAM into large sundae glasses and pour over the chocolate sauce. Finish with the caramelised nuts.

BANANAS WITH RUM SAUCE AND CHOCOLATE FLAKES

50g butter
1 tbsp honey
6 bananas, peeled
  and halved
2 chocolate flake bars

For the rum sauce
110g butter
110g soft brown sugar
pinch of cinnamon
125ml rum
150ml double cream

SERVES 4

TO MAKE THE RUM SAUCE, melt the butter in a pan. Add the sugar and cinnamon and stir to a smooth paste. Add the rum and cream, bring to the boil and cook for 2–3 minutes to make a smooth sauce. Set aside.

NOW COOK THE BANANAS. Put the butter and honey in a frying pan and heat until smooth. Add the bananas and cook gently until soft. Serve with the rum sauce and crumble the chocolate flakes on top. Good with vanilla ice cream.

FRENCH TOAST WITH CARAMELISED APPLES

This is perfect as a breakfast dish or a dessert and particularly good served with a dollop of crème fraîche.

50ml double cream
2 eggs
25g sugar
pinch of cinnamon
100g butter
4 slices of brioche
fresh strawberries or
blueberries, for serving

For the caramelised apples
50g butter
3 Braeburn apples, peeled,
cored and quartered
50g caster sugar

SERVES 4

FIRST PREPARE THE APPLES. Melt the butter in a pan and heat until it is bubbling. Add the apples and stir until they start to colour. Add the sugar and continue to stir until the apples caramelise. If the mixture gets too thick, add a little water to loosen the caramel and cook for another 5 minutes.

IN A BOWL, whisk together the cream, eggs, sugar and cinnamon. Heat the butter in a frying pan. Dip the slices of brioche in the cream and egg mixture until it is well coated, then remove and let any excess drip off.

FRY THE SOAKED BRIOCHE in the butter until golden on both sides. Serve with the caramelised apples.

RHUBARB TRIFLE

8 sponge fingers
2 tbsp sweet sherry
500g rhubarb
50g butter
50g sugar
1 x 500g tub of ready-made
fresh custard
250ml double cream
flaked almonds, to garnish

SERVES 6

PUT THE SPONGE FINGERS in a small bowl, add the sherry and set them aside to soak. Cut the sticks of rhubarb into pieces about 5cm long. Heat the butter in a frying pan and gently sauté the rhubarb until it is soft. Add the sugar and stir well, then leave to cool.

PUT THE SOAKED SPONGE FINGERS in the bottom of a serving bowl. Pile on the cooked rhubarb and add the custard. Whip the cream and spoon on top of the custard.

SPRINKLE with flaked almonds to finish.

HONEY AND MASCARPONE SEMIFREDDO

This is my version of this classic semi-frozen dessert and can be made up to a week ahead. Just make sure you take it out of the freezer and let it defrost slightly before serving so it slices more easily. Be sure to use a good flavoursome honey – it makes all the difference.

3 eggs, separated
120g caster sugar
40g acacia honey
400g mascarpone
375ml double cream

SERVES 4-5

USING AN ELECTRIC WHISK, beat the egg yolks with half the sugar and the honey until airy, creamy and pale in colour. Set aside while you make the meringue.

TO MAKE THE MERINGUE, put the egg whites and the rest of the sugar in a stainless steel bowl set over a pan of simmering water. Whisk slowly until warm to the touch. Take the bowl off the heat and continue to whisk until the meringue forms and the mixture has cooled.

PUT THE MASCARPONE into a separate bowl and add 75ml of the cream. Stir together well, then add this to the egg yolk, honey and sugar mix prepared earlier. Mix carefully so as to keep everything as light and fluffy as possible. Add the meringue and fold it in gently.

WHIP THE REMAINING CREAM to soft peaks and stir into the mixture. Freeze in one large bowl lined with cling film or smaller individual ones overnight. Remove from the freezer 15 minutes before serving, then turn the semifreddo out and slice or serve in scoops.

STRAWBERRY GRANITA

180g sugar
500g ripe strawberries,
    hulled
grated zest and juice of
    1 lemon
small handful of fresh basil,
    chopped
freshly ground pepper
aged balsamic vinegar

**MAKES ABOUT
1.2 LITRES**

PUT THE SUGAR into a saucepan with 250ml of water and bring to the boil. Pour this syrup into a blender, add the strawberries and blend until smooth. Add the lemon zest and juice to the strawberries and blend for another minute.

POUR THE MIXTURE onto a non-stick metal baking sheet and place it in the freezer to cool down. Check it every 30 minutes and as soon as it starts to freeze, keep breaking it up with a fork, stirring the frozen edges into the middle. After approximately 3 hours you should have a flaky, icy substance.

COVER THE GRANITA with cling film and put it back in the freezer. When you are ready to serve, scoop it into a chilled bowl and finish with basil and freshly ground pepper. Add a few drops of aged balsamic vinegar to each serving.

ORANGE SORBET

Sorbets are wonderfully refreshing and good to serve as a change from cream or ice cream. Lovely by themselves or served with other dishes.

250g caster sugar
1 tbsp fresh sliced ginger
½ cinnamon stick
4 oranges
grated zest of 1 lemon
2 tbsp Cointreau

SERVES 4

PUT THE SUGAR, ginger and cinnamon in a pan with 250ml of water. Bring to the boil and cook for 5 minutes.

ZEST 2 OF THE ORANGES and add that and the lemon zest to the sugar syrup. Juice all the oranges and add the juice and the Cointreau to the syrup.

PASS THE MIXTURE through a sieve and leave it to cool down completely. Once cold, transfer the mix to an ice cream maker and churn for 20–25 minutes until set. Store in the freezer until needed.

MELON SORBET

This can be made with watermelon, honeydew or charentais or a mixture as long as the melons are sweet and ripe.

450g melon
zest and juice of 1 lime
2 tbsp grappa or vodka
250g caster sugar

SERVES 4

PEEL THE MELONS and discard the seeds. Blend the flesh in a food processor until smooth. Add the lime zest and juice, then the grappa or vodka and sugar and blend for a minute longer.

POUR THE MIXTURE into an ice-cream machine and churn for 20–25 minutes until set. Store in the freezer until needed.

BLACKCURRANT ICE CREAM

200g blackcurrants
juice of 1 lime
75g plain yoghurt
4 tbsp Kirsch
2 tbsp maple syrup

For the crème anglaise
1 vanilla pod
100ml double cream
50g sugar
3 egg yolks
150ml milk

MAKES 750ML

START BY MAKING THE CRÈME ANGLAISE. Cut the vanilla pod in half and scrape out the seeds. Pour the double cream into a saucepan and add the pod, seeds and sugar, then bring to the boil. Meanwhile, beat the eggs in a separate bowl.

REMOVE THE CREAM MIXTURE from the heat and pour it onto the egg yolks, stirring all the time. Add the cold milk and mix well. Pass the mixture through a sieve, then return it to the pan. Place over the heat and stir until it thickens slightly and coats the back of a spoon.

ADD HALF THE BLACKCURRANTS to the crème and mix in a blender. Once the mixture has cooled down, gently fold in the rest of the ingredients, including the remaining blackberries, with a spatula. Churn in an ice-cream machine for 25–30 minutes until set. Transfer the ice cream to a container and freeze until ready to serve.

COFFEE ICE CREAM

This is one of my favourite things, but make sure you use good espresso coffee. There's no point making this with instant – it won't taste good.

200ml double cream
75g coffee beans
2 shots of espresso coffee
100g sugar
6 egg yolks, beaten
300ml milk
4 tbsp Tia Maria

MAKES ABOUT 600ML

BRING THE CREAM, coffee beans, espresso shots and sugar to the boil, then whizz in a blender for 1 minute on a medium speed. Bring the liquid back to the boil and pour it over the egg yolks, stirring constantly. Add the cold milk and continue to mix well.

PASS THE LIQUID through a sieve and add the Tia Maria. Allow the mix to cool down and then pour it into an ice-cream machine and churn for 25–30 minutes until set. Transfer the ice cream to a container and freeze until ready to serve.

BASICS

CLASSIC VINAIGRETTE

20ml white wine vinegar
salt
100ml olive oil
½ tsp Dijon mustard

MAKES 120ML

PUT THE VINEGAR IN A BOWL, season
well and mix until the salt is completely
dissolved. Add the olive oil and mustard,
then whisk everything together.

RED WINE VINAIGRETTE

20ml good red wine vinegar
1 tbsp balsamic vinegar
salt
100ml olive oil

MAKES 120ML

PUT THE VINEGARS IN A BOWL, season
well and mix until the salt is completely
dissolved. Add the olive oil and whisk
everything together.

SHORTCRUST PASTRY

I like to use half butter and half lard in
shortcrust for the best texture, but use
all butter if you prefer.

170g plain flour, plus extra for dusting
pinch of salt
45g butter, chilled and cubed
40g vegetable shortening or lard, chilled and cubed

MAKES 250G

PUT THE FLOUR and a pinch of salt into a
large bowl. Add the butter and shortening or
lard and rub in with your fingertips until it
resembles crumbs. Add 4–5 tablespoons of
cold water and use your hands to mix it into

a dough. Wrap in cling film and chill for
15 minutes.

BASIC TOMATO SAUCE

4 tbsp olive oil, plus extra for drizzling
1 onion, finely chopped
2 x 400g cans plum tomatoes
1 garlic clove, finely chopped
2 tsp tomato purée
pinch of sugar
1 rosemary sprig

MAKES 4–6 PORTIONS

HEAT THE OLIVE OIL in a pan over a medium
heat, add the onion and cook for 5 minutes,
or until soft and translucent.

ROUGHLY SQUASH THE TOMATOES with
your hands or a fork. Add them to the pan
along with the garlic, tomato purée, sugar
and rosemary. Lower the heat and simmer
for 25–35 minutes, or until the sauce is
thick and has a jam-like consistency.

REMOVE THE ROSEMARY and finish with
a drizzle of olive oil. Store in the fridge for
up to 4 days or freeze.

CHICKEN STOCK

3.5kg raw chicken bones
2 onions, roughly chopped
3 celery sticks, roughly chopped
2 leeks, roughly chopped
1 head of garlic, sliced in half horizontally
3 black peppercorns, slightly crushed
salt

MAKES ABOUT 2 LITRES

PUT THE CHICKEN BONES in a large pan
and cover with water. Bring to the boil, then
reduce the heat and simmer for 45 minutes,
skimming off any fat and impurities as
often as you can.

ADD ALL THE VEGETABLES and the garlic and peppercorns to the pan and simmer for a further 1½–2 hours. Check the seasoning and add a little salt if necessary. Continue to taste and simmer until you feel that the flavour is right. Pass the liquid through a muslin-lined sieve. This stock can be used right away, stored in the fridge for up to 3 days, or frozen.

FISH STOCK

2 tbsp olive oil
1 onion, roughly chopped
1 celery stick, roughly chopped
½ fennel bulb, roughly chopped
1 leek, roughly chopped
1 head of garlic, sliced in half horizontally
5 fennel seeds
3 white peppercorns
2 thyme sprigs
1 bay leaf
500ml white wine
2kg fish bones, plus any fish trimmings
¼ bunch of fresh chervil, stalks only
¼ bunch of fresh parsley, stalks only
salt

MAKES 3 LITRES

HEAT THE OIL in a large, heavy-based pan. Add all the chopped vegetables, garlic, fennel seeds, peppercorns, thyme, bay leaf and some salt. Cook, stirring, for 5 minutes, or until soft and aromatic but not coloured.

POUR IN THE WINE, turn up the heat and boil until the liquid has reduced by half. Add the fish bones (not the trimmings) and enough cold water just to cover. Bring to the boil again, then reduce the heat and simmer for 20 minutes, regularly skimming off any scum.

ADD THE HERB STALKS and cook for another 10 minutes. Remove from the heat, add the fish trimmings and cover. Leave to infuse for 5–10 minutes, then pass through a muslin-lined sieve. This stock can be used at once, stored in the fridge for up to 48 hours, or frozen.

VEGETABLE STOCK

If you don't want to make this amount of stock, reduce the ingredients by half. However, stock does freeze well and you can divide it up into smaller portions for storing.

5 leeks, cut into 2.5cm cubes
20 carrots, peeled and cut into 2.5cm cubes
10 onions, cut into 2.5cm cubes
10 celery sticks, cut into 2.5cm cubes
½ bunch of fresh tarragon, stalks only
½ bunch of fresh basil, stalks only
½ bunch of fresh chervil, stalks only
5 star anise
10 white peppercorns
10 fennel seeds
750ml white wine
1 lemon, sliced

MAKES 6 LITRES

PUT ALL THE VEGETABLES into a large pan and add just enough water to cover. Bring to the boil, reduce the heat and simmer for 8 minutes.

ADD ALL THE HERB STALKS, the star anise, peppercorns and fennel seeds and simmer for another 2 minutes.

REMOVE FROM THE HEAT, add the wine and lemon slices. Allow the stock to cool completely, then refrigerate for 24 hours to allow all the flavours to infuse. Strain before using.

INDEX

ACKNOWLEDGMENTS

Huge thanks to everyone who's been involved in this project. First, Sarah Lavelle, who commissioned the book and left it in the hands of the wonderful Hannah Knowles while she went off to have her baby, Tilly. I'm very grateful to you both for your patience and support. Many thanks, too, to Alex and Emma at Smith & Gilmour for their superb design, Jonathan Lovekin who made the photo shoots such fun and still came up with the best pictures. He's the most brilliant food photographer I know and the only one who has the patience to cope with my chaos. I love him. I'd also like to thank Jinny Johnson for editing the text and plaguing me with questions over many cups of tea and cheese sandwiches, and Lisa Harrison, best-ever home economist, who tested many of the recipes and always gives me such great advice and support. As for Diego Cardoso – I couldn't live without him. He runs the kitchen at Murano and helps with so many other things – he keeps me sane. Thanks, too, to all the staff at Murano – keep up the good work.

And last but not least, thanks to my mum and all the rest of my family and friends. Love you all